Never too Old
to Play Tennis

and Never too Old to Start

Mansfield Latimer

BETTERWAY BOOKS
CINCINNATI, OHIO

Acknowledgments

Books such as this one depend upon the help of many individuals. I want to acknowledge the help of the following: Jack Staton, Doug Crary, Bill Collins, Gene Ray, Herman "Bubba" Ratcliffe, Doug Patton, George Reynolds, Walt Cavanaugh, Henry Smith, Cyrus Schelly, Duane Garver, Paul Graebner, Carl Swensson, Heyward Belser, Howard Jones, John York, Wyatt Dodd, and Ruth Dodd.

Many of the above may be surprised that they contributed to the material in this book. However, playing tennis with them, listening to their advice and suggestions, and just watching them play was the source of much of the information in this book.

My thanks also to Bob Hostage, of Betterway Publications, Inc., who encouraged me to write the book and offered many helpful suggestions. Also thanks to Mary Sproles Crescimanno, Associate Editor, for her help in editing the book, and to the other people at Betterway Publications, Inc. who helped with the book.

Cover design and cover photograph by Susan Riley
Text photographs by Mansfield Latimer
Typography by Park Lane Associates

97 96 95 94 93   5 4 3 2 1

Library of Congress Cataloging-in-Publication Data

Latimer, Mansfield
    Never too old to play tennis, and never too old to start / Mansfield Latimer.
       p. cm.
    Includes index.
    ISBN 1-55870-288-1 : $12.95
    1. Tennis for the aged. I. Title.
GV1001.4.A35L38   1993
796.342--dc20   92-37946
                                            CIP

This book is dedicated to my loving wife,
Catherine.

Although not a tennis player, she has always
supported me in my tennis playing.
Often she has changed her own plans so that
she could accompany me when I played in
tennis tournaments. Her encouragement has
frequently been the extra edge I needed to win.
She is a "Super Senior Wife."

Foreword

Never Too Old to Play Tennis is a book written especially for the older tennis player. In addition, it provides tips and suggestions that can help players from the beginner to the experienced tournament player.

Many older individuals think they are too old to play tennis or to start to play tennis. The information in this book should convince them that they are never too old to play tennis—or to start to play.

I have known Mansfield over the years as a ranked senior player who continues to play in senior tournaments. He is a student of the game of tennis, and in this book he shares the knowledge he has acquired through personal experience and interviews with many of the top ranked senior players.

Each chapter in the book offers special suggestions and instructions on different aspects of the tennis game.

The index makes it easy to find the specific instructions that will help you improve your game. When these are followed, your entire game will improve.

I've enjoyed reading this book and feel you will also. If you read a few of the suggestions each time you are ready to play a match, it won't be long until their execution will be second nature. That's when you will become the winning tennis player you've always wanted to be.

And remember, *you're never too old to play tennis — or to start to play tennis*.

—Jack Staton
Winner of sixty-eight national tennis titles and "grand slams" in the 70, 75, and 80 age divisions.

Left, Jack Staton.
Right, Mansfield Latimer.

About Jack Staton

Jack Staton, who wrote the Foreword for this book, is proof of the premise that one is never too old to play tennis — or too old to start to play tennis.

He did not start to play tennis until he was thirty-one and now, in his 80s, he is still playing—and winning—senior tournaments.

Jack's personal record is exceptional. He has won sixty-eight national tennis titles and has also won "grand slams" in the 70, 75, and 80 age divisions.

He is an outstanding example of what one older player achieved when he continued to play tennis. Not every older player will be able to duplicate Jack's success as a tennis player, but his playing can serve as an inspiration to other older players and encourage them to continue to play tennis—or to start to play tennis.

About the Author

Mansfield Latimer has been playing tennis for sixty-five years. He won his first tournament in 1935 and continues to play in ten to twenty tennis tournaments each year. He has held national, southern, and state rankings and is currently ranked number one in South Carolina in the age 75 division. He has also won five tennis gold medals in the Florida Senior Olympics.

Mansfield owned and operated a business consulting firm and was an active public speaker. He sold his business fifteen years ago. Since then he has devoted his time to playing tournament tennis, travel, and writing fiction. His writing to date includes numerous articles and five books.

He lives in Rock Hill, South Carolina and spends the winters in Florida playing the Florida Senior Tennis Tournament circuit.

Contents

Introduction

According to the United States Tennis Association, at least 700,000 Americans over the age of fifty-five play tennis on a regular basis. Many of these senior tennis players are in their 70s and 80s. Some are even in their 90s. You can be one. You are never too old to play tennis.

This book was written to encourage older tennis players to continue playing and to encourage other seniors to learn the game. The purpose of the book is to consolidate in one publication advice on how to play winning tennis and to cover other information that is of special interest to senior players.

There are many "how to" books on the market that furnish instructions on how to grip the racket and hit the ball. Many of these books are very good for beginners, and the average player can improve his game by reading them. This is not a "how to" book. If you are a beginning tennis player, I suggest that you explore your library for "how to" books to help you learn the basics. This book will still be of use to you, especially if you have other sources on hand to refer to with questions.

There is more to playing *winning* tennis than just being able to hit a tennis ball. If you want to play winning tennis, you must also know the *who, what, where, when,* and *why* of the game. You will find the answers to these "w" questions in this book.

The material for this book has been accumulated through observation, study, and interviews, and by playing tennis for more than sixty-five years. Much of the advice has been around since the game of tennis was first played, so you may have read or heard many of these tennis tips before. But even if they are common knowledge, they can—when followed diligently—enable you to become a better player.

Football, basketball, and many other games are played by young people. Tennis, however, is known as a "lifetime" sport and is played not only by young people, but also by older people. It's unfortunate that many adult players think that the "lifetime" part of tennis has expired when they reach the age of forty or forty-five and they stop playing tennis. This decision deprives them of many years of enjoyment playing the game they love.

Also, it really is never too late to start playing tennis. A survey of senior tennis players found that 35 percent didn't begin to play tennis until they were adults. A prime example of a player who got a late start playing tennis is Herman "Bubba" Ratcliffe of Atlanta, Georgia. Herman did not start to play tennis until he was *seventy years old*. At the age of eighty, he and his partner won the national senior Grand Slam in the eighty age bracket.

So, if you play tennis, don't stop just because you're getting older. And if you have never played tennis, it's not too late to start. I hope this book provides the information and inspiration you need to continue—or start—to play.

1

Senior Tennis Players

Do you think you are too old to play tennis? While age is one factor to consider, it is not the most important. It's not your age that determines whether you can, or should, play tennis. Age is merely the yardstick that's used to determine how many years you've already lived.

AGE

It is your physical — and mental — conditions that determine whether you can play tennis. We all know people who are "old" at thirty and others who are "young" at sixty. There is nothing you can do about your age as a number, but there is a lot you can do to maintain and improve your attitude and physical condition.

As you get older, certain physical changes occur in your body: "stiffness" in the connective tissues increases; "wear-and-tear" weakens joints; and muscle strength decreases with disuse. Increasing muscle strength around an injured joint may help protect it from excessive stress.

Fortunately, many of the physical problems commonly associated with aging are really signs of inactivity. These problems can be minimized, prevented, or even reversed by exercise. The older a person is, the more important it is to get in the good physical condition that comes from a regular program of exercise. There are specific tips in the chapters on physical condition and exercise to help you counter the physical effects of aging.

Not too many years ago, there was a popular saying, "Life begins at forty." If this is the case and you are eighty years old, your life began only forty years ago and your actual age is only forty. I know a lot of eighty-year-old players who play tennis as if they were only forty. Playing tennis is one way to remain young at heart.

PLAYING SENIOR TENNIS

If you have played tennis for many years, it is natural that you want (and try) to continue playing the same type of game you played when you were younger, but this is not possible. As you age, you will have to change your game strategy to fit your physical condition.

You must recognize your limitations and understand what you can and can't do physically. If you have many years of experience, you should be able to "out-think" most younger players. Experience is a great teacher. The problem is that by the time you get the experience, you may be too old to take full advantage of it. You can always use this experience to offset some of your physical limitations. That's why so many older players can beat younger players. Although you may not be as fast as you once were, you should be able to hit the ball better because you ought to understand both yourself and the game better.

Of course it smarts to lose to a younger, less capable player whom you could have defeated 6-0, 6-0 when you were his age. But you are still playing tennis, aren't you? All is not lost, just a game or two.

Some senior players are now playing the best tennis of their lives because they are playing "smart" tennis. If you're a senior player, take advantage of your experience. Play percentage tennis by using the shots you "own" at the right time to the right place. You may be surprised how many "kids" you can defeat.

While it is important to maintain a young mind and heart, as a senior player you must remember that you don't have the physical condition and stamina of your youth. That makes it especially important for you to husband your strength. You must be careful how you expend your limited store of energy. You must learn to spread your energy over the entire length of the match without hurting your game. If you "run out of gas" too soon, the game is over. It will not help you at that point to be able to out-think your opponents. Your body will not respond if you have used all of your energy.

There are several ways senior players can conserve energy while playing interesting, winning tennis. One mistake seniors make is getting involved in long rallying duels. Many seniors, and some younger players, are so steady they can keep the ball in play forever. This type of game saps their limited physical resources. What you should do in a case like this is to go for a winner (winning shot) a little sooner than you normally would.

If you are a senior player, consider switching to an oversize

Note oversize racket.

racket. Oversize rackets have a larger "sweet spot" and will give you more power. More and more players are now playing with oversize widebody rackets. The adjustment to the larger racket is mostly psychological as the physical adjustment is minimal.

The secret of playing winning tennis when you get older is the desire to play. Playing more with other older players who don't hit a ball a "hundred miles an hour" will help you maintain that desire. If you are a senior who is just starting to play, try to find other older players to play with. They will not only help you improve your game, they will increase your desire to play more and more often.

IMPROVING YOUR GAME

The first step to improving your game is to have *realistic goals*. Realize that you are not making your living playing tennis and that you will never be able to play like the young professional tennis player who devotes all his or her time to tennis. Understand who you are and what you will be able to achieve considering your own strengths and limitations.

You should have both short and long range goals; goals that you expect to accomplish in one month, one year, five years, etc.

Players after finals of 75s tournament. Note long pants and wooden racket of winner.

End of final match of 75s tournament.

It would be really nice if we could achieve all of our goals. But life isn't like that. Everyone has limits—some more than others. What you *can* do is to do the best you can at whatever you try.

Set realistic goals and once you have reached them, set new goals. Your goals should be *specific*, not general. Without a specific goal you have no yardstick to measure your improvement. Without specific goals, you won't be able to improve your game. When you set your goals too high, you are headed for disappointment and frustration. Do the best you can with the ability you have—in tennis and in other areas of your life.

One realistic goal should be to *increase the number of times you can keep the ball in play*. If the average number of times you can safely return the ball is three, try for four. When you can consistently return it four times, try to raise your level to five times, then six, then seven, then eight, etc. Your wins will increase in direct proportion to the increase in the number of times you can safely return the ball.

Almost every player would win more often if he could do one thing: duplicate the relaxed execution of his practice strokes when playing a match. Make this one of your goals. One way to reach that goal is to try to carry into the match the same relaxed mental attitude you have when you practice. When you are able to do this you will be a winner.

Review your goals on a regular basis. Set new goals as the old ones are reached. Your ultimate goal should be to enjoy yourself (and to win), not to look good.

SUPER SENIORS

In addition to the 700,000 Americans over the age of fifty-five who play tennis on a regular basis, there are approximately 2,300 dedicated senior tournament players. These are called "Super Seniors."

We have completed a detailed survey of 100 of these Super Seniors. They were interviewed at various tournaments where they were playing. They live in twenty-six different states and their ages range from fifty-five to eighty-nine.

The information secured in these interviews is not only interesting, but the answers to many of the questions will encourage senior players to continue to play. The responses may also encourage those who have never played tennis to start to play. You might consider these Super Seniors your role models.

The questions asked during these interviews cover a broad

range of categories. The responses are presented in a question-and-answer format. The answers to most of the questions are given as percentages to better present the overall picture of these Super Seniors.

The results of the survey are as follows:

Age *At what age did you start playing tennis?*
65 percent between 6 and 21—average starting age, 12.
35 percent between 21 and 70—average starting age, 46.
Total number of years played ranged from 11 to 70. However, 46 percent had some hiatus periods when they did not play tennis due to time in the military or for business or personal reasons. These periods ranged from 5 to 30 years.

Practice *Who do you practice with?*
57 percent practice with younger players.
25 percent practice with both younger and older players.
18 percent practice with older players.
Have you ever taken tennis lessons from a pro?
36 percent said they had taken lessons.

Games and *How often do you play tennis?*
Tourna- The average number of times was four times a week although 14
ments percent actually play seven times a week.
How many tournaments do you play in each year?
Number ranged from 1 to 37.
The average was 13 tournaments.
Have you ever won a tournament?
All respondents but one had won a tournament.

Ranking *What was your best ranking?*
STATE State ranking ranged from 1 to 9.
81 percent had at one time held a state rank.
DISTRICT District ranking ranged from 1 to 6.
63 percent had at one time held a district rank.
43 percent had at one time been ranked number 1 in the district.
NATIONAL National ranking ranged from 1 to 41.
86 percent had at one time held a national rank.
5 percent had at one time been ranked number 1 in singles.
10 percent had at one time been ranked number 1 in doubles.
One player had won 62 national singles titles.
2 players have won grand slam doubles titles.

Style of *What type of game do you play?*
Play 55 percent play an all court game.
35 percent play a backcourt game.
10 percent play a net game.
What stroke do you use?
38 percent hit flat.
32 percent slice the ball.
30 percent hit with topspin.
Only 54 percent hit *exclusively* with one type of stroke, since 46
percent hit with some topspin (usually forehand) and with
some slice (usually backhand) and some flat.
Do you have a two-handed backhand?
Only three percent hit their backhand with two hands.
Do you play left-handed?
5 percent play left-handed. One player who is left-handed plays
right-handed tennis.
Do you use drop shots?
80 percent use drop shots.
Do you use lobs?
90 percent use lobs.
How many aces do you average serving in a match?
Number of aces ranged from 0 to 10 (average was 2).
How many double faults do you average serving in a match?
Number of double faults ranged from 0 to 6 (average 2).

Rackets *What racket do you use?*
59 percent play with Wilson rackets, with Wilson Profile being
the most popular.
24 percent play with Prince rackets.
17 percent play with other rackets.
What size racket do you play with?
60 percent play with 110.
How many rackets do use?
Average was 4 plus (one survey respondent owned 14 rackets,
11 of them different).
How often do you buy a new racket?
Average was slightly over one per year.
At what tension is your racket strung?
42 pounds was the lowest.
80 pounds was the highest.
60 pounds was the average.
What type of string do you have in your racket?
63 percent use synthetic gut.
25 percent use good grade of nylon.

Note support on both knees of this top-ranked player.

2 percent use gut.
How often do you have to have your racket restrung?
53 percent restring once or twice a year.
47 percent restring only when a string breaks.

Health *How do you rate your health?*
60 percent—excellent.
30 percent—good.
10 percent—fair.
What physical problems do you have currently or have you had in the past?
55 percent—knee problems. 4 had knee operations.
34 percent—eye problems. Most are minor but 5 have had cataract operations, 2 have glaucoma, and 1 player is blind in one eye.
29 percent—shoulder problems. Some expressed it as bursitis.
24 percent—back problems.
24 percent—elbow problems.
13 percent—wrist problems.
11 percent—hip problems. 3 had hip operations.
10 percent — some heart problems. Most minor, although 2 have had heart attacks, 3 have pacemakers, 3 had open heart

surgery, and 1 had a heart valve replacement. One player was playing tournament tennis again six months after having open heart surgery,

7 percent—skin cancer.

5 percent—ankle problems.

4 percent—arthritis. It is possible that some of the other listed joint problems may be caused by a degree of arthritis.

4 percent—diabetes.

1 percent—sinus condition.

From the above statistics you may get the impression that these Super Seniors are a bunch of sick invalids. Actually, most of them are in relatively good condition—much better shape than they would be in if they weren't playing tennis.

Those who *do* have physical problems are coping with them in a positive manner that enables them to continue to play tennis. If you are experiencing similar problems, these Super Seniors should be an inspiration to you. You too can continue to play tennis. If you do, not only will you have fun but both your physical and mental health will improve. So don't give up!

Supports *Do you wear any kind of medical support?*

13 percent—knee support.

8 percent—elbow support.

2 percent—back support.

Do you wear glasses to play tennis?

55 percent do not wear glasses to play but do wear glasses to read.

45 percent wear glasses to play.

Do you smoke?

None of the players interviewed were currently smoking.

58 percent have never smoked.

42 percent smoked at one time but have quit.

Average time since they stopped smoking is 23 years.

Other *Did you ever play competitive sports other than tennis?*
Sports 97 percent said yes. Sports played were/are as follows: baseball, basketball, football, track, soccer, hockey, softball, squash, boxing, handball, skiing, bowling, swimming, rowing, and wrestling.

Only 3 said that they did not ever participate in other competitive sports — these Super Seniors have always been athletes, even those who started playing tennis late.

Exercise *Do you have a regular exercise program other than playing tennis?*

Only 55 percent follow any regular exercise program other than playing tennis. This was a little surprising since it's generally agreed that you don't play tennis to get in shape, but you get in shape to play tennis. Perhaps so much tennis doesn't leave time for other kinds of exercise.

Some of the exercise programs of those who do exercise are as follows: stretching, lifting light weights, jogging, walking, riding a stationary bike, aerobics, ice skating, and using a ski machine.

Business or Profession The Super Seniors represent thirty-five different businesses and professions. Some with multiple representation are: doctors, engineers, lawyers, military personnel, teachers, and tennis pros.

Retirement *How long have you been retired?*

Longest length of retirement was 30 years.

Average length of retirement was 12 years.

Shortest length of retirement was 1 year.

Advice Since these Super Seniors have had many years of experience playing tennis, it seemed appropriate to ask them for some advice for other senior players, both beginning and experienced. The questions and their answers follow:

If you had to give one bit of advice to beginning players what would it be?

TOP THREE ANSWERS Take lessons from a registered professional.

Have fun.

Practice.

OTHER ADVICE Start with the correct grip.

Think.

Learn to serve first.

Learn the correct strokes.

Hit the ball against a wall.

Play a lot.

Concentrate.

Stay with it.

Be patient.

Don't try to kill the ball or you will make errors.

Live a good clean life and stay off drugs.

Play three times a week.

Enjoy the people you play with.

Keep your eye on the ball.

Try to be consistent.

Learn an all-around game.

Follow through on ground strokes.

Finally, play because you want to, not because someone else wants you to play.

If you had to give one bit of advice to other senior players what would it be?

TOP THREE ANSWERS

Stay in shape.

Stretch before playing.

Enjoy it.

OTHER RESPONSES

Play for your health.

Play in moderation.

Wear glasses if needed.

Pace yourself.

Don't overdo it.

Practice.

Hit back one more time than your opponent.

Try to be steady.

Accept defeat gracefully.

Don't let bad calls upset you.

Don't take tennis too seriously.

Try to improve your strokes.

Don't give up.

Keep trying.

Hope to survive.

Buy the best equipment you can.

Keep playing even if you have personal or business problems.

Unless you learned to volley as a junior, stick to a baseline game.

Seniors don't need advice.

And finally, one said, "Quit playing so I can win."

2

Successful Aging

As individuals age, their bodies naturally sustain a certain inevitable amount of wear and tear. The good news is that age alone is not the single determining factor in an individual's ability to function and/or enjoy life. Many physical problems are preventable and some are reversible.

The real culprit, in most cases of mild disability, is an unhealthy lifestyle that causes disabling conditions in the elderly, including frailty and immobility, as well as serious chronic diseases. According to the University of Texas' *Lifetime Health Letter*, "Lack of exercise, poor diet, and bad habits, like smoking and excessive drinking, contribute more than anything else to infirmity."

The University of Texas Health Science Center at Houston publishes this newsletter monthly. Recently, they covered the subject of aging. They provide valuable information on the physical characteristics of aging and some ways to keep those changes in check by simply keeping active and following a healthy diet. The good news is, it's never too late to do something about the process of aging.

An active, healthy old age should be enough of an incentive to persuade you to do the things you should and stop doing the things you shouldn't do. And the extra bonus is that you can continue to play tennis. As illustrated in the chapter on "Super Seniors," there is no reason why either age *or* mild physical problems should affect your ability (or desire) to play winning tennis.

The rest of this chapter is quoted, with permission, from the *Lifetime Health Letter*, Volume 4, Number 2, dated February 1992.

IT'S NEVER TOO LATE

Medical experts agree that a healthy lifestyle can keep most people vigorous and independent into old age. Moreover, it can help prevent or delay many chronic diseases like cancer, heart disease and stroke.

Here are some physical characteristics and abilities that may change as the body ages—and some ways to keep those changes in check by simply keeping active or following a healthy diet:

Muscle mass. After age 45, muscles tend to shrink and fat moves in to fill the space.

But strength training can keep muscles strong, allowing you to get around easily no matter how old you are. Moreover, it's never too late to reverse the decline in muscle strength and size.

Research at Tufts University has shown that even people in their 90s can triple their strength and increase muscle size 10% after just eight weeks of strength training, according to Tufts researchers William Evans, Ph.D., and Irwin Rosenberg, M.D., co-authors of *Biomarkers: The 10 Determinants of Aging You Can Control* (New York: Simon and Schuster, 1991).

Heart function. Several changes take place in the heart as people age. Cardiac output—the amount of blood the heart can pump —decreases. In addition, during exercise, heart rate doesn't increase as much as it does in younger people. For a 20-year-old, peak heart rate is generally 200 beats per minute; for a 60-year-old it's closer to 160, say Drs. Evans and Rosenberg.

But the heart adapts by pumping out a larger volume of blood with each beat, enough to meet the demands of exercise. Keep in mind that a low-fat diet and exercise can help prevent heart disease.

Aerobic capacity. Aerobic capacity—the body's ability to process oxygen in a given time—starts to decline as early as age 20 in men and in the early 30s in women. A 65-year-old's aerobic capacity typically is 30% to 40% lower than that of a young adult, according to the Tufts team. That means an older person gets out of breath with considerably less effort.

But the decline occurs much more slowly among people who exercise regularly. An older individual can maintain aerobic capacity, but has to work harder to do it.

Overall physical performance. It's true that the average 60-

year-old can't run as fast or throw as far as the average 25-year-old. But the fit person who's 80 often can do better than a sedentary person half that age.

Bone density. With age, bones gradually thin, often leading to osteoporosis and a higher likelihood of fractures. The process occurs both in men and women, although bone loss accelerates in women after menopause, and women have smaller bone size to begin with.

But a number of studies have shown that regular weight-bearing exercise like walking, running and cycling can reduce the rate of bone loss. Exercise also improves the body's ability to absorb calcium, say the *Biomarkers* authors. Getting at least the recommended dietary allowance of calcium (800 milligrams a day) and, for postmenopausal women, taking estrogen can help keep osteoporosis at bay.

Metabolism. Basal metabolic rate, or calorie expenditure at rest, falls about 2% per decade starting at age 20, according to Drs. Evans and Rosenberg. Therefore, an average 70-year-old needs 500 fewer calories a day to maintain weight than an average 25-year-old.

But the authors say older people's reduced muscle mass is almost wholly responsible for the gradual reduction of basal metabolic rate. Maintaining muscle mass through strength training can help keep metabolic rate up and weight down.

Blood sugar. With age, the body's ability to use sugar from the bloodstream declines, causing blood sugar levels to rise. That increases the risk of diabetes, which can be fatal if not controlled. Some researchers suspect that excess blood sugar may contribute to the aging process itself.

But excess body fat, a high-fat diet and inactivity are stronger contributors to the problem than age is. A low-fat, high-fiber diet can increase cells' sensitivity to insulin, especially when combined with regular exercise workouts, the Tufts researchers note.

Immunity. The immune system "tires" with increasing years, becoming less efficient. By the time people reach old age, they have 15% fewer T cells, immune system cells that mobilize the body's defenses against invading organisms. But the biggest factors in immune system impairment are changes in the T cells themselves, which make them less able to respond in times of need. The higher incidence of infections in elderly people is believed to be the result of these changes.

But researchers suspect that proper nutrition helps keep the immune system strong. Foods rich in vitamins C and E and beta-carotene are thought to be particularly important.

Blood pressure. As people age, blood pressure tends to increase, posing a greater danger of heart disease and stroke. *But* the increase often is due to excess weight and bad health habits. For most people, exercising regularly, keeping weight under control and not smoking can help keep blood pressure down.

Nutrient levels. The body's ability to absorb calcium declines with age, disrupting the body's calcium balance. Levels of vitamins D, B2, B6, B12, zinc and other nutrients also appear to drop, say Drs. Evans and Rosenberg.

But eating a healthy, balanced diet should supply enough nutrients to meet the body's needs. If not, supplements can make up the difference.

Susceptibility to chronic diseases. The elderly are more likely to get osteoarthritis, Alzheimer's disease, cancer, heart disease, stroke and autoimmune diseases, such as rheumatoid arthritis.

But several important lifestyle changes can significantly reduce your risk of many of these diseases.

Reduce excess body weight and exercise regularly. Obesity and inactivity contribute to many chronic and potentially fatal diseases.

Don't smoke. And drink only in moderation. These habits contribute to high blood pressure, stroke, heart attack and dementia.

Follow a healthful diet. A low-fat diet helps prevent heart disease, stroke and cancer. Certain nutrients, such as vitamins C and E, beta-carotene and calcium, appear to protect against cancer.

Fortunately, the conditions that pose the biggest threat to independence and an active lifestyle in the later years are the things we have the most control over. Keeping active, following a healthy diet and dropping bad habits can yield benefits that make life well worth living through a ripe old age.

3

Psychological Aspects of Aging

The preceding chapter on successful aging covered ways to avoid or reverse many of the physical problems associated with growing older. In addition to these physical problems, there are psychological problems that sometimes coincide with aging. In this chapter we cover ways of coping with some of the psychological aspects of growing older.

As seniors, we need to redefine the way many look at old age. In many ways, old age is a time of opportunity. With many of life's major responsibilities over — the children put through college, job insecurity a thing of the past—older people are finally free to pursue interests they have pushed aside for years. For many, tennis is included in this list of interests.

The aging process brings with it new challenges in addition to new freedoms. Confronting these issues and coming to understand and accept the potential losses associated with aging can free a person to enjoy the positive qualities of the later years. Coming to grips with these challenges can help make the golden years among the very best of life. Moreover, older individuals typically are wiser and more self-confident than they may have been in earlier years.

The University of Texas' *Lifetime Health Letter* has given us permission to quote from their March 1992 issue covering certain coping mechanisms that can help you handle the psychological problems of growing older.

COPING MECHANISMS

According to Barry Lebowitz, Ph.D., chief of the National Institute of Mental Health's aging research branch, there are three basic strategies that can help people approach the stresses of aging constructively. These strategies are to anticipate, to get as much information as possible, and to mobilize social support.

Anticipate. "It helps to prepare as much as possible for a perhaps foreseeable event like retirement or a spouse's death. Being prepared can help soften the impact and speed adaptation."

Get information. "Knowledge really is power. It enables understanding and facilitates decision-making. In short, knowledge makes you feel more in control, whether the issue involves something as serious as a friend's cancer or something less threatening, such as coming to terms with wrinkles or thinning hair."

Mobilize social support. "Family members and friends give moral support and direct assistance and may be able to help you in times of crisis."

Myths. "Don't buy into the myths of old age. It's never time to slow down or settle into the rocking chair, unless you want to, says Ellen Brubeck, M.D., a Mount Olive, NC family physician. 'Try to live to your full potential at any age,' she advises."

Stay active. "Keeping on the move will help you feel good about yourself and help you maintain independence through a ripe old age."

What better way to stay active than playing tennis? Playing tennis can help you live up to your full physical and mental potential at any age. And the people you play tennis with can also help you mobilize social support.

Lead a healthy lifestyle. "You'll feel better and possibly avoid many of the diseases associated with aging."

Some suggestions on how to lead a healthy lifestyle are covered in Chapter 2, Successful Aging.

Cultivate plenty of lifelong interests. "Hobbies or intellectual pursuits, such as reading, gardening, painting, genealogy, flyfishing or woodworking, can sustain you in difficult times and keep you from feeling lost when life circumstances change."

Socialize regularly. "Mingling and sharing with others lifts your spirits, builds self-esteem and staves off loneliness. Moreover, some studies suggest that strong social ties may be important to your physical health as well."

What better way of doing these last two than playing tennis? Tennis is truly a lifelong interest and by its very nature it requires regular social interaction.

Have a positive, enthusiastic, attitude. "An upbeat approach to life will draw others to you. Some studies suggest that a positive attitude can extend life, notes Dr. Brubeck. Even if it doesn't, you'll have a better time during the years you have to enjoy.

"Health care professionals have begun to recognize the value of a positive view of life as they observe that some older people cope well and lead active lives despite serious illnesses while others with less severe conditions become alienated, isolated and inactive. State of mind can make all the difference."

"The whole idea, of course, is to age gracefully. Coping effectively with the challenges and side-stepping the pitfalls along the way help make successful aging possible."

Proof of this can be found in the chapter on Super Seniors. Despite the fact that a majority of the players are affected by physical problems (some serious), they continue to play and enjoy tennis. You can too if you have a positive and enthusiastic attitude and learn how to play around your physical challenges.

What better way to do all of these things than playing tennis? You stay active; you lead a healthy lifestyle; you socialize regularly; and you maintain a positive and enthusiastic attitude. Remember, you are never too old to play tennis or to start to play.

4

Physical Condition

Your greatest ally in a tough match is physical condition. No tennis player can play winning tennis unless he is in good physical condition. If a player is not in good condition, his skill level is of no use to him, as he will be unable to successfully execute the skills he has learned.

If a player is badly outclassed, his good physical condition will not win for him, but if the skill level of the two players is close, the player who is in the better physical condition will win. This is particularly true in long grueling matches where endurance becomes a key factor.

When you play in hot weather, stamina is an especially important factor. Many a match played under broiling sun has been decided more on physical condition than on ability.

Physical limitations and fatigue limit the number of shots you can make and affect your accuracy. Pace yourself for endurance. This is especially important for older players.

BODY TYPE

Many people wonder if there is a best body type for a tennis player. There really is not. A look at some of the best players in the history of tennis will make this readily apparent. There have been short players like "Bitsy" Grant and tall ones like Bill Tilden. Some have been skinny and some have been stocky. Obviously, some have been male and some female. There is the argument that tall players, both male and female, have an advantage when it comes to serving. Their added reach does give some advantage in hitting the ball over the net when they serve. However, even if they may have a serving advantage, they can still be defeated by shorter players.

INJURIES

Injuries can be the tennis player's number one enemy. This is especially true for older players and those who are not in good physical condition.

Most tennis players get hurt because they are not in good physical condition. Lack of practice and exercise are invitations to injury. If you get in better shape *now*, you are not as likely to get hurt later.

Pros are supposed to be superb athletes, but I don't know of a single pro who has not, at some time in his or her career, been injured. It is little wonder, then, that older players and out-of-condition players often sustain debilitating injuries.

When it comes to injuries, prevention is the best strategy. This is especially important for older players because older bodies heal more slowly. The best way to avoid injury is to build *extra muscle strength*. This is why exercise is so important, especially a strength training program. This will greatly reduce the chance of your getting hurt—plus, it will improve your tennis game.

Good flexibility helps protect muscles against pulls and tears. Flexibility refers to the ability of the joints to move through a full range of motions. Older individuals are often stiff for a variety of reasons. The primary reason is simply inactivity. If you continue to use and move your joints and muscles, they will remain strong and flexible.

Knee and foot injuries are the bane of older players. The culprit in most cases is the hard court. The pounding your body takes on hard courts can cause damage to your feet and knees over a period of time. This damage can be reduced or avoided by playing on hard courts in moderation and by using extra padding in your shoes when you do play on hard courts.

Never ignore pain. Listen to your body. It is trying to tell you something. Pain is nature's way of telling you that you're hurt. Listen to this message. Find out what's causing the pain. Then take appropriate action — rest and treatment. That way you'll be back on the court sooner.

The old saying "no pain, no gain" should be "*when in pain, no gain.*" When you over-exercise or exercise when in pain, you may find that you are plagued by muscle soreness and aching knees. At best, instead of feeling refreshed after a workout, you may feel fatigued.

Don't try to "play through pain." Contrary to what some say, trying to play through pain is the worst thing you can do.

Ignoring pain won't make it go away and will probably only aggravate it.

Minor injuries can be treated by the RICE formula: Rest, Ice, Compression, and Elevation. Any major injuries, however, should receive immediate medical attention. See your doctor. Don't try to "work it off." You will just cause further injury.

Don't return to playing tennis until the injury has healed completely. This is especially important for senior players.

DIET

Good diet is just as important to good physical condition as exercise and possibly even more to good health.

Good eating habits and proper diet do not begin at courtside. The strength and stamina needed to play winning tennis are determined by your diet and exercise during the months prior to your walking on the court to play.

There are certain foods you should avoid immediately before playing tennis. Conventional wisdom repeatedly advises us that foods high in fat or protein can cause cramping and bloating. In addition, sugary drinks taken within an hour of playing can impair muscle performance. It is best not to eat anything within two hours before playing.

Eating during playing is not a good practice unless you are feeling weak. If you feel lightheaded or weak, you may want to eat or drink something light—but not much, since food tends to stay in your stomach. Proper eating prior to your match should prevent the above problem. Eat a balanced meal a few hours before you play and you should have plenty of energy to sustain you through the match.

DEHYDRATION

While eating is not advisable during play, drinking fluids is. Dehydration is something that can happen in any active sport if proper steps are not taken to prevent it. This is especially true when temperatures soar into the 90s.

Unfortunately, you cannot depend on Mother Nature to tell you when to drink water or how much to drink.

So what should you do to avoid dehydration? First, you should drink a lot of water *before* you start to play. Second, you should drink some fluids at every *changeover* during play.

What to Drink There is no doubt that what you need to avoid dehydration is fluid. What fluid should you drink? Most people agree that water is the fluid of choice. Some sports drink proponents recommend beverages such as Gatorade, Exceed, Max, etc. They claim that these sports drinks replenish the fluids lost during exercise and replace carbohydrates and electrolytes. Other nutritionists claim that sports drinks contain too much sugar. And of course they cost money.

You can decide what you prefer—water or a sports drink. But the important thing is to drink before play, during play, and —don't forget—*after* play.

There is only one kind of fluid to avoid—alcoholic beverages. Alcoholic beverages have an especially negative impact on the body and also impair judgment and promote urination, which increases dehydration.

COOLING DOWN

Cooling down after a game is just as important as warming up before a game. Slow down gradually, stretch gently for five or ten minutes, and drink a lot of fluids. Not only can this stretching slowdown reduce muscle stiffness, but it can prevent an abrupt drop in blood pressure that occurs when you suddenly halt vigorous activity. Movement in cooling down is especially important in the case of older players. Never stand still immediately after vigorous exercise.

5

Exercise

Life isn't measured just in years. What really matters is the *quality* of life. One must keep physically fit to lead a physically active life—and to play tennis. "Exercise helps healthy people better adapt to stress, and it improves self-esteem. People feel better about themselves," says Andrea Dunn, a postdoctoral fellow in psychology at the University of Colorado Health Sciences Center. Exercise can yield dramatic benefits to the human body and spirit. Also, people who maintain their fitness are about a third less likely to develop high blood pressure.

QUALITY OF LIFE

Regular exercise can substantially improve four basic elements of physical fitness: cardiovascular endurance, muscle strength, muscle endurance, and flexibility—all necessary if you are to play tennis. Be sure to consult your physician before beginning any exercise program.

Too many people say, "I ought to get in better shape," but never do anything about it. Regular exercise can make you more calm, less anxious, more confident, and more healthy. In addition, it sharpens mental flexibility and short-term memory.

Lack of a regular exercise program poses a major risk of physical injury to older players. Well-toned muscles help prevent injuries.

CONDITION

If you are to play tennis you must be in good physical condition. The older you are, the more important physical condition becomes.

No matter how talented a player you are, you will never be a

Good exercise!

consistent winner unless you are in good physical condition. You need more stamina than your opponent. As play progresses and you become tired, not only will it be more difficult for you to get to the ball, you will begin to make more and more unforced errors.

In the heat of summer, conditioning is often the difference between winning and losing. If you are losing a final set tiebreaker you may think it's due to lack of mental toughness. That's possible, but it is more probable that a lack of good physical condition is affecting you. Winning big points at the end of a match comes from the stamina that is a result of being in good physical condition.

If you become tired or winded during a long rally, take as much time as you can between points—without stalling or violating the continuous play rule.

AEROBIC TRAINING

Playing tennis is good exercise, but it shouldn't be your only exercise. You need a non-tennis exercise program to get in the best possible physical condition—both to play your best tennis and to avoid injury.

A stop-and-go sport like tennis doesn't keep your heart rate elevated to an aerobic rate. The oft-cited maximum heart rate formula is: 220 minus your age. For example, if you are sixty years old, your maximum aerobic heart rate would be 160 (220 less 60). If you are seventy, your rate would be 150, and so on. If you want the effect of aerobic training, you need an exercise program in addition to tennis. Try jogging, cycling, swimming, or any other activity that provides you with sustained periods of aerobic training.

INTERVAL TRAINING

The traditional recommendation for exercise has been to work out at a moderate rate for twenty to forty minutes. Recent research suggests, however, that you may be able to get in shape faster with *interval training*—spurts of intense exertion alternating with low-intensity recovery periods. Interval exercise can be used for almost any type of exercise.

When exercising at a steady speed there is a gradual slowing down as the workout continues. The interval training method makes it possible to maintain intense exertion, knowing that a low-intensity period is coming up. The intense periods let you work out longer at your optimum heart rate, so your muscles receive the greatest amount of oxygen.

This type of interval training works well as you practice your tennis. The slower recovery period of interval exercise also allows for the removal of some lactic acid that accumulates in the muscles and makes them tired. An extra bonus to interval training is it's less boring than a steady-pace exercise. Thus you are more likely to stick with your exercise program.

SKELETON

The skeleton is governed by the same principle that governs every organ in the body: use it or lose it. The major task of the skeleton is to provide structural resistance to the constant force of gravity.

The bones of the skeleton are constantly changing and remodeling in response to different forces. They get stronger if needed and begin to dissolve if not used. If you stay in bed for just twenty-four to forty-eight hours, your body immediately begins to dump calcium out of every bone in your body.

When a broken arm or leg is immobilized in a cast, the fracture heals, but this immobilization causes the entire bone to lose enormous amounts of calcium and it is weakened in the process. Fortunately, when the limb is pressed back into service, the bone quickly regains calcium and strength.

You want strong bones? Start walking. Walking is superior to bicycling and swimming for strengthening bones because of its weight-bearing nature—though swimming and cycling are certainly healthy. In general, if you strengthen a muscle, you strengthen the bone along with it.

Note the following:

Your legs were made for walking
And unless that's what you do
One of these days your legs
Are going to snap right under you!
And then you can't play tennis anymore.

DON'T OVER-EXERCISE

As we have just discussed, being in good physical condition is a prerequisite to playing winning tennis. Be careful, however, not to let your desire to get in good condition cause you to push yourself too hard. Beware of *over-exercise*. Just because working out three times a week brings you good results does not mean that six times a week will be twice as good.

Your body needs some time off to recuperate from strenuous exercise or play. Exercise is good *and* it is necessary—but don't overdo it. Follow a sensible exercise program. Remember to consult your physician before beginning an exercise program.

STRETCHING

Contrary to what you may have heard, stretching is *not* the smart way to start your exercise. Stretching cold muscles can injure them. It's essential to *warm up first*, then stretch. Any warm-up activity that circulates the blood to joints and muscles is fine. These include mild jogging, stair climbing, and walking.

When you exercise any muscle, do it slowly. Avoid fast, jerky, or bouncy moves.

To improve your flexibility, after warming up your muscles, perform slow, static stretches until you feel a pulling sensation—not pain—in the center of the muscle. Hold the stretch for ten seconds (working up to twenty to thirty seconds)—don't bounce, relax, and then repeat. Stretching should be gradual and relaxed—never bounce. Bouncing can tear muscles.

WEIGHTLIFTING

If you are serious about getting in the best possible condition, you should consider lifting weights. Many pros, male and female, are now recognizing the importance of a weight training program. The extra strength helps them play better and longer because they are not as likely to get injured. If lifting weights is good for the pros it can also be good for you.

It seems weightlifting is especially helpful for women. Studies show that exercise that exerts pressure on the bones helps to strengthen them. This helps women avoid the bone thinning that affects so many after menopause.

Lifting weights gives you the muscle strength and endurance necessary to improve your performance in any cardiovascular game. One main benefit, however, is that your body is much better able to cope with the stress that occurs in tennis when your opponent does something that causes you to twist and turn suddenly. The extra strength keeps you from getting hurt.

If you think you are too old to start a program of weightlifting, you are wrong. The reasons for taking up strength training—also called resistance training—are compelling.

Experts now realize that strength training is critical for total fitness. In fact, strength has now been added to fitness guidelines, which previously focused almost exclusively on aerobics.

The more muscle in your body, the better off you are. The problem is that after the age of forty-five, muscle strength deteriorates rapidly, up to forty percent by age sixty-five. Weightlifting is one way to slow—or even reverse—this deterioration.

William Evans, Ph.D., Chief of the Human Physiology Laboratory at the U.S. Department of Agriculture's Human Nutrition Research Center on Aging at Tufts University in Boston, had this to say about strength training in a recent issue of the University of Texas' *Lifetime Health Letter*.

"Many of the changes associated with growing old result mainly from immobility rather than aging. And they can be largely prevented or reversed through strength training. Muscle strength training can do more to improve overall conditioning than anything else.

"Strength training also has a positive effect on bone," he says. "Because muscle mass appears to correlate with bone mass, strength training probably is superior to weight-bearing exercise like walking for preventing osteoporosis.

"In the very old, strength training may not have an appreciable effect on bone. But the muscle strength and better balance that come with training can prevent falls, which are directly responsible for a good percentage of bone fractures," says Dr. Evans.

"Another benefit of strength training is that it promotes weight control in two ways: the exercise burns calories and training creates more muscle and less fat in the body. Greater muscle mass boosts metabolism (which tends to slow with age) and thereby speeds calorie burning.

"'It's never too late to start a strength training program,' says Dr. Evans. In a study he coauthored, 87- to 96-year-olds showed dramatic improvements from training. By the end of eight weeks, two people no longer needed to use a cane to walk. All 10 people in the study experienced three- to fourfold increases in strength.

Safety What about safety? Even in Dr. Evans's study of very old people with a variety of medical conditions, strength training caused no health problems. The fear that strength training puts extra stress on the heart is simply unfounded.

In fact, strength training is establishing a foothold in the rehabilitation programs for heart attack patients, which have traditionally focused on achieving cardio-respiratory fitness through aerobic exercises. It turns out that weak muscles limit a patient's ability to complete the aerobic exercise necessary to maintain a healthy heart.

If you decide to start a strength training program, you may want to join a health club with free-weights and weight machines. Trained employees can offer advice on correct form and safety, and they can help you get the most out of your workout.

In addition, there are a number of good books, such as Dr. Evans's book *Biomarkers*, which can provide you with instructions on correct weightlifting exercises. You don't even have to buy weights. Dr. Evans suggests using plastic milk containers filled with sand or water for your upper body workouts. Plus, an at-home program is more convenient—and cheaper.

The following are not intended as instructions for a strength training program, but are merely safety suggestions (adapted from University of Texas' *Lifetime Health Letter*):

- Get your doctor's approval before starting any exercise program.
- It is important to warm up for at least five minutes by moving then stretching to circulate the blood to muscles and joints. The warm-up reduces the chance of muscle strains.

- The American College of Sports Medicine recommends the amount of weight lifted should be 60% to 80% of the maximum weight you can lift once. This will enable you to do eight to twelve repetitions of each exercise.
- Don't try to do too much—especially in the beginning.
- If a joint or a muscle starts hurting, stop what you are doing.
- After exercise, cool down with stretches to avoid soreness and muscle tightness.
- Wait at least two hours after a meal before exercising.
- Schedule a day's rest between exercise sessions to give muscles time to recover.

Strength training reverses the downhill slide in muscle strength that comes with aging and leaves so many older people frail and dependent. Weight training is the best, time-tested way to tone and strengthen all muscle groups. It will add another dimension to your fitness regimen.

Weight training's immediate rewards are a noticeably firmer and stronger body. And over the long term, it will help you to enjoy an active, healthy life throughout old age.

And isn't that your goal?

6

Eyes

Bobby Riggs can wear an overcoat, carry a suitcase in one hand, wear only one shoe, and still beat most tennis players except Billie Jean King. But blindfold him and he couldn't beat Grandma Moses. That's because the eyes are the secret of athletic success. Blindfold the number one player and he couldn't even function as a ball boy.

If your game is suffering, your eyes may be part of the problem, especially if you are an older player.

When an older tennis player's game begins to falter, the reason most often given is, "the legs are the first to go." This may be the case, but remember, the eyes may be the first to go just as often.

The eyes undergo changes with age. Vision becomes less efficient as you get older. Throughout life the lens (the flexible, transparent portion of the eye) becomes increasingly thicker and more rigid. With age, the pupil, which controls the amount of light entering the eye through the lens, becomes smaller. Vision suffers as a result of these changes.

Because some of these changes come on gradually, many people do not realize that deteriorating sight is affecting their tennis game.

Problems with eyesight are not limited to the older player. Usually the young player's legs are still good, but this is not always true of the eyes. Martina Navratilova illustrated this for us. When her game began to suffer it was discovered her eyes were the problem. When she started to wear glasses, her game returned to its former level.

Overexposure to sun rays while playing tennis can damage your eyes. Minimize this risk by wearing a cap or visor and perhaps sunglasses with UV protection.

EYES AND STRESS

There is another problem you may experience with your eyes, even though you have 20/20 vision. We have all had occasions when we stumbled on a step or ran into something. We probably didn't realize it at the time, but the chances are it happened when we were under some kind of stress. The connection between such accidents and stress has long been accepted on the basis of common sense, but now two researchers have added a scientific explanation.

Longevity magazine reports that Mark B. Anderson, Ph.D., of Beloit College and Jean M. Williams, Ph.D., of the University of Arizona have made a study of the correlation between psychological stress and how much we see with our peripheral vision.

Their study revealed that the more stress an individual was under, the more likely he was to have relatively narrow peripheral eyesight when forced to respond quickly to a visually demanding task.

Dr. Williams gives the following advice to persons under pressure: "Maximize your concentration since you may be missing critical cues in your peripheral vision, like judging the distance between you and a moving car."

This advice is equally good for the tennis player who may be missing critical cues in peripheral vision when judging the distance between his racket and a moving tennis ball.

If you are under stress, there is need for extra concentration. The best solution, of course, is to try to eliminate stress, or at least control it. There are some tips on this in Chapter 8.

VISUAL JUDGMENT

Dr. Leon Revien, director of the Athlete's Visual Skills Training Center in Great Neck, NY says, "Outside of mental errors, almost 100 percent of the mistakes an athlete makes stem from visual misjudgment. If you reduce your visual misjudgments, your performance will improve." Keeping your eyes on the ball can do more to ensure your athletic success than all else combined.

Some individuals do have better eyesight than others. Ted Williams' eyesight was so good when he was at the peak of his career that he was able to see a baseball as it approached the plate better than most players. His superior eyesight—and his skillful use of it—helped make him one of the greatest baseball players of all time.

KEEP YOUR EYES ON THE BALL

When it comes time to play a point, *keep your eyes on the ball*. Watch the ball as it comes off your opponent's racket; as it approaches; as you hit it; as it goes back.

Forget about the match, the point, the score, and your opponent. Just concentrate on the ball. Your stroke should be an automatic one previously programmed during practice.

While your opponent is hitting the ball, watch him as well as the ball. But once he has hit it, *watch only the ball. Always* watch the ball instead of looking in the direction you want to hit it. When hitting, look for the seams on the ball. This is a great way to increase your concentration. You may not be able to see the seams, but you will be forced to concentrate directly on the ball if you try this.

If you don't keep your eyes on the ball, you may be defeated by a less gifted player who does—no matter how good your vision.

If you are not blessed with 20/20 vision, are you doomed to playing a second-rate game? Of course not. Having 20/20 vision simply means that you can focus clearly on a small object twenty feet away. Eye-hand skills are independent of this figure. If you have poor vision, you can always acquire glasses or contact lenses to correct the deficiency.

EYE EXERCISE

Most encouraging of all are studies which show that vision is a *learned skill*. Dr. Revien says, "By working at it you can improve your ability to use your eyes." Vision therapy is not complicated. It can be practiced with or without props.

Dr. Donald Getz of Van Nuys, California, chairman of the American Optometric Association Sport Section, suggests a vision therapy exercise that is easy to understand. In this exercise, attach a tennis ball to the end of a string and tie the other end of the string to a support about eye level. Start the ball swinging back and forth. Keep your eyes on it without thinking about it. After you have done this for some time, start the ball swinging in a circle instead of back and forth and continue to keep your eyes on it.

As you watch the ball it is important that you follow the movement only with the eyes. Do not follow its movement with your head. Every time you move your head, you disturb the balance system. The same is true when you actually play tennis.

Try to follow the ball as much as possible with the eyes only, without moving your head.

When you become proficient at keeping your eyes on the *entire ball*, take a felt pen and mark an X on the ball. Then, instead of trying to look at the entire ball, concentrate on the X. This is the principle discussed above and can really be a help when you are playing tennis. Instead of looking at the entire ball, try to follow the seams, the rotation, or the lettering. This will ensure that you keep your eyes on the ball.

Don't be lazy about this exercise. Concentrate. Put other things out of your mind. Keep *both* eyes on the ball.

Billie Jean King uses a version of this exercise. Before a match, she holds a tennis ball in her hand and stares at it for fifteen minutes. This is her method of getting in the proper frame of mind to keep her eyes on the ball when actual play begins. Of course, there is no guarantee that you will be able to play like Billie Jean if you do this exercise, but if it works for her, it probably won't hurt you.

These suggested exercises will help make watching the ball second nature. The more automatically you watch the ball, the more of your conscious concentration you free up for other aspects of the game. If you have to think about keeping your eyes on the ball, other things may go wrong.

Dr. Revien summed it up when he said, "Vision is a learned skill. It can be enhanced by working at it." Remember every sport starts with the eyes—and ends with the eyes.

VISUALIZATION

Dr. Jack Liberman, a Miami optometrist who does vision therapy for athletes says, "One of the simplest, most worthwhile of eye exercises is one that can be done without props at any time you have a few spare minutes." It is called *visualization*.

All you have to do is close your eyes and use your imagination. Picture, in your mind's eye, that your opponent is about to serve to you. See his racket hit the ball. Watch the ball as it comes toward you. Try to see the seams on the ball until your racket hits it. Continue to see the ball until finally, in your mind's eye, you win the point.

One of the fringe benefits of visualization is that you never have to lose a point. This additional psychological bonus reinforces your belief that you can win and adds confidence to your game.

Remember, the eyes are the secret of athletic success.

7

Psychological Aspects of Tennis

Tennis is both a mental and physical game. At times the mental aspect can be even more important than the physical aspect for both you and your opponent. You need to be aware of the effects on your opponent and yourself so that you can use this information to your best advantage.

PLACEBO EFFECT

Most individuals do not realize the power the mind can exert over the physical body, yet we are surrounded with examples of this power. The effect of placebos is a common example of the power of the mind over the body. Almost everyone is aware of experiments in which harmless, unmedicated preparations, such as sugar pills, are given to patients who are told they are receiving medication. These patients know what the medicine is *supposed* to do, and in many cases their bodies will respond in the same way as the patients who were given the actual medication.

As the placebo effect illustrates, we often get what we expect. If our belief is strong enough, it becomes a self-fulfilling prophecy. Positive thoughts make you more likely to experience positive results. Winners expect to win—and they usually do.

To be successful you have to think success. The process of visualization is a good example of this power. If you visualize yourself hitting the ball correctly (improving your strokes), your strokes will improve. Belief is essential to creating improvement.

SUPERSTITION

Many players are superstitious. Typical behavior might be wearing a specific item of clothing (a lucky hat), avoiding stepping on lines, using a certain brand of balls, etc.

Superstition becomes a mental crutch that may actually help the player—when he's winning. He may think, or even say, "I'm winning because I'm wearing my lucky hat." However, when he is losing, this superstition can hurt him. Then he thinks, "I'm losing because I forgot my lucky hat." The problem is not the hat. The danger lies in his not recognizing that the reason he is winning or losing has nothing to do with his "lucky hat," but is dependent on his skill level and that of his opponent and on whether or not he is playing his best game. Superstition must never take the place of practice and good strokes. If a player begins to rely on superstition, it becomes more than a game; it becomes destructive to his outlook and self-definition. In this way, superstition is an insidious mental condition that can creep up on an individual without his realizing it. Guard against this compulsive behavior.

Routines It is important that you do not confuse routines with superstition. There is a major difference between the two. For example, a player may bounce five times before he serves. This is merely a routine that helps the player to avoid tension and stress. This type of routine can have a positive influence on a player's game.

CHOKING

Tennis players call it choking. Golfers call it the "yips." It's also known as the "twitches," "staggers," "jitters," and "jerks." Regardless of what name it goes by, almost all athletes experience it sooner or later. Obviously, choking begins with a psychological response.

Researchers have now conducted studies of this phenomenon and discovered some reasons why players choke and what happens to muscles that actually cause the problem.

The Mayo Foundation for Medical Education and Research in Rochester, Minnesota, has given us permission to quote the following from the April 1990 Mayo Clinic Health Letter. Although this was specifically addressed to golfers "yips," this information sheds some light on the subject of tennis and choking.

. . .many neurologists now recognize the yips as a form of focal dystonia (dis-toh'nee-ah) — a sudden, involuntary contraction of a muscle or a group of muscles. . . .

The exact cause of the yips is yet to be determined. Such factors as age, previous injury and obsessive-type personality have all been implicated. Researchers reporting in the journal Neurology *surveyed 335 golfers, 28 percent of whom said they have been bothered by choking. The typical survey respondent was about 50 years old and had played golf for 30 years or more.*

Researchers speculate that, in some golfers, the condition may result from biochemical changes in the brain that accompany aging.

This theory of aging being the cause of choking does not explain why young players also experience this problem. It's possible, of course, that these biochemical changes in the brain occur even in the young.

The Mayo study also shows that, "Excessive use of the involved muscles, and intense demands of coordination and concentration may make the problem worse." In addition, previous injury and obsessive-type personality have all been implicated.

Competitive play seems to increase the incidence of choking. Stress is a factor in all involuntary movement disorders, including choking. This would seem to be true, since players seldom experience choking during practice. Choking occurs most often during serious play and most frequently during tournament matches when anxiety is present.

The Mayo letter indicates that the problem of choking "does not disappear when players take prescription medication to relieve anxiety."

In addition, the study found that, "Choking may spread to involve other parts of the body, such as the arms, shoulders, legs, feet, neck, jaw, or even the eyelids." If this is the case, it is easy to understand how involvement of other parts of the player's body would adversely affect the execution of his tennis strokes.

Researchers examined the thought patterns of people who choke. They found the condition more common among players who think unwanted thoughts or have images that interrupt concentration before a stroke.

Since choking can be the bane of serious tennis players, what can be done to eliminate the problem? Unfortunately, at this time there is no real cure for choking. Choking is mental. Fear of making errors leads to choking. Tension while playing crucial points may cause errors.

One reason you choke is the fear of losing makes you so tense that you no longer hit your own shots. This is especially true when you are losing to someone you feel you should be able to beat.

Choking can also be caused by becoming tentative once you have the lead. You want to protect your lead, so you back off and wait for your opponent to lose. You start playing too cautiously instead of continuing to play the game that put you in the lead.

Negative thinking that gives you an excuse for losing can cause you to choke. Similarly, thinking about the past instead of the present can make you choke.

You are not likely to choke when hitting your most comfortable strokes. You are more likely to choke when forced into situations that call for strokes you are not confident with.

Everyone chokes at some time—even pros. Avoid choking by keeping your mind on the match. Relax and take deep breaths. Keep playing, and chances are, the tension will pass.

There is a vaccination against choking. It's called confidence. It doesn't prevent choking altogether; it will make the choking attack very mild with quick recovery. Keeping unwanted thoughts and images out of your mind and maintaining concentration is the best approach to this problem. Some players report that choking can subside of its own accord, only to return intermittently.

With this in mind, it might be helpful to view choking as just another hazard of the game. But isn't that just one of the things that makes tennis such a challenging sport?

Panic Attack A panic attack is the fear felt by a person who is afraid of something that is not literally, physically dangerous. The fear is so real to the person that he is unable to function in a normal manner. It is a mental condition that causes fear without any logical basis in reality.

Perhaps this is analogous to the choking experienced by tennis players. There is no real physical danger to the tennis player, just as there is no real danger to a person who suffers from a panic attack.

Here are some rules I have formulated from personal observation and reading for coping with panic attacks. I feel that these suggestions can be of assistance to the tennis player who is having consistent difficulty with choking.

- Remember that although your feelings and symptoms are frightening, they are neither dangerous or harmful.
- Understand that what you are experiencing is merely an exaggeration of your normal reactions to stress.
- Do not fight your feelings or try to wish them away. The more willing you are to face them, the less intense they will become.
- Don't add to your panic by thinking about what "might happen." If you find yourself asking, "What if . . . ?" ask yourself, "So what?!"

- Stay in the present. Be aware of what is happening to you rather than concern yourself with how much worse it might be.
- The next time you choke, think of these rules for coping with panic. They should help you cope with your choking.

Remember, the mental part of your game will help only if it is backed up by your stroking ability. It's not enough just to know what to do, you also have to be able to execute your strokes correctly.

POSITIVE AND NEGATIVE ATTITUDES

Many players, when they get a lead, start thinking, "How am I going to avoid losing?" instead of "Now I can close out this match." This negative thought reversal is one reason many players lose.

When two players are of equal ability, you would expect most games between them to be close. But often this is not the case. There will be some one-sided games no matter how closely matched the players are. More often than not, the difference can be attributed to the mental attitudes of the players on those given days. When the positive thinker loses a point, he becomes increasingly determined to win the next point. When the negative thinker loses a point, he becomes discouraged and is more likely to lose the next point — and the next and the next. Avoid this pitfall. Adopt a positive attitude and *play to win every point*.

Forget about winning and losing. Whenever you worry on the court it means you are not concentrating. Play for the sheer fun of playing. Relax and enjoy the game. When you do this the chances are you'll stop losing and start winning.

Sooner or later everyone is going to lose. Whether it's a point, a game, or a match, how you cope with losing will determine if it becomes a regular pattern or something to motivate you to improve your game.

FRUSTRATION

For many players, the greatest stumbling block to winning tennis is frustration. One of the premier causes of frustration is trying to make shots or moves that you don't "own." In other words, attempting things you have not practiced enough to be comfortable with. Frustration also comes from setting unrealistic goals you already know you have no chance of reaching.

Often the difference between winning and losing is the difference between the frustration level of the two players. It takes a lot to frustrate a player with a high frustration level. The higher your frustration level, the better your chance of winning the point—and therefore the game.

The most frustrating opponent is the baseliner who can keep the ball in play forever. His strategy is to try your patience and frustrate you to the point that you will try to make a low-percentage shot in an effort to end the point. The best response to the strategy of the steady baseliner is patience. Continue to rally with him; try *his* patience. He can't hurt you from the baseline. Sooner or later, he will hit a short ball you can attack, or make a mistake to cost him the point.

Another tactic to use against the frustrating baseliner is to draw him to the net with short, angled shots or drop shots. This will place him in unfamiliar territory, which can give you the advantage. If you are not comfortable with this shot, practice it. You will be confident in using it against this strategy in the future and will save yourself a lot of frustration (and points).

If you want to play winning tennis, find ways to keep your frustration at "low tide."

TIPS TO YOUR ADVANTAGE

Mental Toughness Mental toughness is concentration brought to bear on the point you are playing. It includes positive thinking, an indomitable attitude, extra physical effort at the time it's needed, and the confidence that you will win. Mental toughness keeps you from losing by simply giving up. Positive mental images can help you perform under pressure when you are playing a crucial point.

The average club player will never attain either the physical condition of the pro or his stroke expertise. But the average player does have the potential to approach the mental level of the pro. What club players should do is try to attain the pro's mental level. Every player has the potential to improve the mental level of his game.

Often it is not the player with the best strokes who wins, but the one who has the mental edge. Athletic success is more than physical strength and skill. The head should be used as much as the feet.

Mental Discipline Mental discipline helps avoid errors. Don't let yourself think about anything that can have a negative impact on your game.

You may not be able to keep the birds from flying over your head, but you can keep them from lighting in your mind. You may not be able to keep anxious or negative thoughts from entering your mind during a tennis match, but you can—and must—keep them from controlling and dominating it. Just notice them and let them drift out of your mind.

Your mind can only do one thing at a time. You should concentrate on what is happening in the game and on moving your body to the proper position. If you are telling your body what to do, you can't be thinking about what might go wrong. Your body will do what you tell it to do, but you must communicate with it.

Weak mental preparation can be more disastrous than weak strokes. Guard against feeling that what ultimately happens in a match is beyond your control. If you start thinking negatively, you will become discouraged and your game will suffer. Avoid negative "self-talk." Always prepare yourself to play your best game. This will help keep you encouraged and playing strongly.

The average player tends to blame all his mistakes on mechanical or physical errors. These may have occurred, but the question is, what *caused* the mistakes? Did you commit an error because you were not concentrating or because you were not prepared? The primary cause of most errors is the lack of proper *mental* preparation. The physical skills will not help you if your mind is not focused.

The Sub-conscious Many of our capabilities are determined by that part of our mind of which we are not aware—the subconscious. You should practice your strokes so much that they come naturally—that you no longer have to consciously think about every minute detail and movement. You should become familiar with your strengths and weaknesses so that you unconsciously move toward your strengths in any given situation. Let your unconscious reactions feed the computer of your mind so you can sort out the probabilities of success or failure in a given situation.

The pianist doesn't have to think which key to hit; and the typist performs nearly "unconsciously" on the typewriter. Of course, they didn't begin with this level of ability. They had to practice first. The same thing is true of the tennis player. He must practice until his skill at hitting the ball is like the skill of the typist hitting a typewriter key.

Your goal should be to reach the level of performance where hitting the ball is done without thinking. Then and only then will you be able to concentrate on the *end* and not the *means*.

**Visuali-
zation**   As you prepare to play tennis, give yourself time to visualize yourself playing your best, most relaxed, most focused and successful game. Visualization is a powerful tool that can improve your tennis game. It is a process of creating pictures in your mind. You *see* what you want to happen and at the same time you *believe* that it will happen.

Many players do not understand how and why visualization works. Visualization is thinking in visual images instead of words. Perhaps if the word "imagination" is substituted for "visualization," it will be easier to understand. What you do is imagine *what* you want to happen and *see* it happen in your "mind's eye." It has been shown that you have a better chance of performing well if you picture yourself performing well.

Research shows that concentrated mental rehearsal is almost as important as actual practice. Mental images can mobilize the body's natural ability. Imagine yourself hitting a perfect serve, moving to the net, volleying a return, and moving to cover the shot for a winner.

If, in your mind, you can see yourself hitting a perfect forehand, you are more likely to hit a perfect forehand in actual play. Jack Nicklaus visualizes every golf shot *before* he hits it. You should do the same with each of your tennis shots before you have to hit them on the court.

Visualization is a powerful tool. Here are some examples of how visualization has worked for some individuals. Perhaps these examples will convince you of the power of visualization and encourage you to use visualization to improve your own game.

Air Force Colonel George Hall was a POW in Vietnam for five and a half years. At the time of his capture, he was a four handicap golfer who shot in the middle seventies. During the time he was a POW he played an imaginary round of golf every day.

He replayed in his mind the best rounds he had ever played. (This is called reinforcement of success.) He also played imaginary games on every course he had seen on TV.

In his mind's eye he teed up the ball, hit it, saw it land, walked to it, hit it onto the green, studied the break, and putted down.

Upon his release from captivity, Colonel Hall returned to the United States. A few weeks after his return, he played in the New Orleans PGA Pro-Am. He shot a 76 although his physical condition was not good. This was exactly what his handicap had been seven years before.

The news media interviewed Colonel Hall and asked him, "How do you account for your incredible round of golf? Was it luck?"

"Are you kidding?" replied Colonel Hall. "I never three-putted a green in all my years as a POW. By the use of visualization I was able to maintain my skills as a golfer."

World-class track star James Robinson uses visualization to improve his performance. Long before the real race, he is running it in his mind, rehearsing every second of the half-mile as surely as he practiced each day on the track. The image is so clear he can hear his heartbeat, feel the cinders crunching under his shoes, see himself surging near the end, and feel the finish tape snap across his chest. This is visualization at its best.

Successful imagery is not simply visual. It should incorporate sounds—the racket hitting the ball—the ball bouncing—the sound of the crowd—as well as your physical sensations and mental responses.

Visualization is not a cure-all, but properly utilized it is a very important aid to winning a tennis game. It does not, of course, eliminate the need to practice.

Visualizing the act of winning is a necessary prelude to winning. It's more than daydreaming—it's essential preparation.

Think About the Right Things

Many players make the mistake of thinking too much about the wrong things when they play. They start thinking about how to grip the racket, hit the ball, etc. When this happens you shift to "external" thinking. Concentrate on your game plan, not the basic strokes that should be developed during practice.

Don't think about those things that are out of your control. You can't control what your opponent does, but you can control what you do. Make the most of what you do best. Block all distracting thoughts out of your mind so you are mentally prepared to play tennis.

When you are on the tennis court, you spend only about a third of your time performing the physical part of the game. Two thirds of the time is spent in other activities—waiting being the primary "activity." The skills required during this part of the game are mostly mental. This is why the mental part of the game is so important. Focus your mental activity on your skills and strategic thinking, not on emotional issues.

Practice time prior to the start of play is not only the time to warm up physically, but also the time to warm up psychologically. Forget the past and the future. When it's time to play, your mind must be focused on the present—and the ball.

Take a Mental Break Concentrating 100 percent of the time during a match is almost impossible. It actually creates more of a problem because you will become mentally as well as physically fatigued. The best answer to this problem is to take a mental break when you change sides. Allow your mind to shut off totally. When you return to play, you should be mentally refreshed. These small planned breaks in concentration will help you stay sharp when it is most crucial—during actual play.

Remember the impact of the mind on the body. Have you noticed that you feel much more fatigued when you lose than you do when you win? In the game of tennis, as in many other events, fatigue is often a state of mind as well as a physical state. If you are feeling mentally fatigued, never let it show to your opponent. If you are tired, he may be as well. If you show it, he might feel energized by the knowledge that you are wearing down.

Making errors in the final stages of a match is generally the result of both mental and physical fatigue. Avoid this by working on your physical condition and concentrating on mental discipline and relaxation.

Specific Tips
- The first game in any match is always important. If you win it, you gain a psychological advantage over your opponent and a jump on winning the set. The first game is doubly important if you have never played your opponent before. This is the time to play a solid game of percentage tennis. You are both probably a little nervous and you want to keep your opponent that way.

  The first game is not the time to take chances with risky shots. Muscles are still a little tight—despite the warmup. Make an extra effort to keep the ball in play. Establish your rhythm and get the feel of your opponent's game. This is the time to make sure that you are concentrating on what is happening in the particular point being played rather than worrying about what just happened or what might go wrong.

- If you are too proud to play defensive tennis when necessary, your personal psychology is working against you. Defensive tennis is merely keeping the ball in play without taking any unnecessary risks.

- Failing to hit a ball you thought was going out, and having it fall in, not only loses you the point but psychologically affects your play on the next point—or perhaps the next several points. Always try to return the ball unless it is *clearly* out. Each return gives you more confidence and aids you in winning.

- If, during a match you are winning, you begin to mentally compose newspaper headlines about your being the winner, you will be psychologically distracted from playing the game and may start to lose.

- The opposite is also true. Do not be tempted to concede the set to your opponent when you are down 1-4 or 2-5. You are never defeated until the last ball is out of play. Giving up in this way can have both immediate and long-lasting effects on your game.

- Don't slack off if you are favored to win against your opponent. Play your best game, no matter who it is against. Do not allow yourself to get lazy; you will be surprised how many times you will lose if you are over-confident. Remember it is easier psychologically to play your best game against a top player than against a mediocre player. With everything to gain and nothing to lose, you may play "over your head." This helps explain why seeded players are sometimes upset by unseeded players.

- Do not allow yourself to become intimidated by a better player before you play against him. While you want to be aware of the strengths and weaknesses of your future opponents, it may be advisable to scout your opponent just long enough to discover his strengths and weaknesses. If he is playing outstanding tennis and you watch him too long, it may have a psychological effect that could cause you to lose your confidence.

- Some research has shown that an aerobic exercise program can have psychological benefits, including improved self-esteem and lessened anxiety. Obviously, these translate into growing confidence which will help you play winning tennis.

Look Like a Winner The way to play the role of a winner is to *look like a winner*. When a point is over, regardless of the outcome, walk slowly and calmly into position. Even if you don't feel like a winner, you can look like a winner to your opponent—and this impression will affect his game.

It has been said that when actors play roles they sometimes begin to feel they are actually the characters they are portraying. The same thing is true of the tennis player. When you act like a winner, you begin to feel like a winner—and you'll probably be a winner.

The ultimate way to drain your opponent's mental reserve is to convince him you are going to win—and he is going to lose.

TIPS TO YOUR OPPONENT'S DISADVANTAGE

On a tennis court, your opponent's psychological image of himself as a tennis player will be affected by your attitude toward him. If you show him that you are afraid of losing to him, he will feel strong. If you appear confident, he may feel uncertain.

A lot of "psyching" goes on in tennis and the best defense is to *ignore it*. If someone tries to psych you, it will work only if you allow it to work.

For a psych to work against your opponent, it helps to know his weaknesses and how to probe them. The essence of a psych is to make your opponent think and worry. It's less important what he thinks about than that you distract him mentally, get him to think—to lose his focus on the game.

There are definite written and unwritten rules of conduct in tennis, but within these it is legitimate to try to psych your opponent in every way you can. The next few pages contain some examples of legitimate psychs.

Remember, even top pros fault more often on crucial points —match, set, or break point. If pressure can do this to pros, why be surprised if it happens to you? When you are playing one of these points, concentrate so you can be sure your serve will be good. The best way to avoid a double fault is to be sure your *first* serve is good. This is the time to be mentally tough.

The player who hits the fast, error-prone first serve, usually has a feeble second serve. With a "cream puff" second serve to look forward to, the receiver becomes more confident and aggressive. Cleaning up your service will keep you from allowing your opponent this psychological lift.

Two other shots that will improve your psychological advantage are the drop shot and the lob. The mere threat of a drop shot or a lob will have a psychological effect on your opponent. He will begin to wonder if, or when, you will use the drop shot or lob. This can cause him to become anxious, and anything that upsets him is a plus for you.

When you win a long rally, it tends to break down your opponent psychologically and make him impatient the next time you engage him in another long baseline rally. If your opponent is leading and seems eager to finish off the set or match, it is to your advantage to slow down the pace.

There are many other things you can do that will have a negative psychological impact on your opponent.

Body Language The way you carry yourself has a definite effect on your opponent. Be aware of your body language; the way you walk and act. Remember, looking confident can be intimidating to your opponent while sending a message that you are not confident may strengthen his confidence and resolve.

No matter how badly you're playing, hold your head up. Look confident. Don't let your opponent see that you're discouraged or tired. When you look like a winner, you're more likely to become one.

Pressure Pressure builds up during the playing of big points. Even if you win the point, there is a tendency to experience a letdown. There may be a nervous reaction that causes you to miss shots you have been making before with ease. Guard against this.

Try to put enough pressure on your opponent so he is forced into game-losing errors. Being in the defensive position in tennis is a position of pressure. There is a lot more pressure when you are defending than when you are attacking. Do your best to keep your opponent on the defensive.

Put pressure on your opponent by keeping the ball in play. Let him be the first one to take a chance on error by hitting too hard or trying for a placement too close to the line.

If you can win the first two or three games in a match you will be putting pressure on your opponent. This can often lead to victory because of an opponent's inability to pull himself together when he is behind.

Net Play There are many reasons to come to the net, but an important one is often overlooked. This is the psychological effect it has on your opponent. Almost all players, especially club players, are under extra pressure when they see their opponent charging the net. The pressure often results in their making an error.

Net-rushing means exactly that—you *rush* to the net. It would be called net-walking if you were supposed to walk—in which case you would be caught in "no man's land." When you play net, do it wholeheartedly by rushing hard and fast to get in as far as you can. If you stop to see where your approach shot lands, you'll be late getting to the net.

You win at the net not by hitting hard shots but by being consistent and *placing* the ball accurately. When you volley, hit to open court. Don't volley nonchalantly.

Don't stand too close to the net, since this makes it easy for your opponent to lob over you. Once you're at the net, don't back away except in the case of a lob.

There is no law that says you have to come to the net—especially if you have hit a poor approach shot. If your strength is playing from the backcourt, it may not be advisable for you to try to play a net game. Especially if your opponent is good at passing shots and lobs. The net rusher will win or lose quickly.

The bottom line is this: anything that is good for you is bad for your opponent. You want to minimize your own anxiety and increase his. The next chapter talks more specifically about stress and how you can keep it from negatively affecting your tennis game.

8

Emotions and Winning Attitudes

Emotions during a tennis match can be either good or bad, helpful or harmful. They can contribute to your winning or your losing. Properly controlled, they are an asset; allowed free reign, they are a liability. Use your emotions in a positive manner to enhance your court performance.

Emotional stamina is as necessary as physical stamina for your persistence in the face of tough competition. A positive attitude will improve your tennis game. When the difference in skill between two players is small, the mental attitude can spell the difference between victory and defeat.

There may be some things you can't control. For example, you cannot keep your opponent from making a good shot. You can, however, control your emotional response to his good shot. Controlling your attitude will take you a long way toward winning.

In order to enjoy playing tennis you need the right attitude. It's a game; a game that can keep you healthy, make you new friends, and be lots of fun to play. But it's just a game—don't take it too seriously.

STRESS AND TENSION

Stress is a state of mind, a feeling of uneasiness. You feel stress when you feel under pressure and believe yourself powerless to do anything about it.

Stress can also be induced by physical exertion or exhaustion such as is experienced in a long, hard-fought tennis match. Fortunately, recovery from this type of stress is usually much quicker than the recovery from mental stress. In addition, being in good physical condition helps you cope with physical and mental stress.

There are many things that cause mental stress, both before and during a game, but most stress during actual play is self-imposed. Of course, physical distress can cause mental stress as well, but I want to concentrate on the effects of mental stress and how to combat it in your game.

Effects Not all individuals are affected equally or in the same way by stress. Stress produces behavioral changes such as nervousness, tension, and anxiety. It can also cause physical changes such as increased heart rate.

One natural response to stress is to tighten your muscles, thereby creating muscle tension. Even after a stressful situation passes, you may retain muscle tension for hours.

Tension is a mental or nervous strain, often accompanied by muscle tautness. You are likely to be more tense when you are playing someone you feel you should beat than someone you expect to beat you.

Tension prevents your body from doing what it knows how to do and leads to muscle tightness beyond appropriate levels.

It would be easy to understand why you might be nervous or scared and under tension had you entered a rodeo and were about to ride a bucking bronco. In that case you might get hurt, but why be nervous or scared before or during a tennis match? It's only a game, and you're not going to get hurt. The worst thing that can happen to you in a tennis match is you'll lose. Remember this and you won't have to be as worried about tension.

Not all stress is necessarily negative. It's only when stress and tension get out of control that they cause problems. If you can harness your stress, it can help you by creating energy. A certain level of nervousness can actually improve your concentration and performance. If you feel no stress at all, you are bound to be too relaxed to perform at your best.

Being nervous can energize you. This is nature's way of preparing you for combat and telling you that you are ready. The problem is in controlling your nerves. Channel your nervousness into positive action and it can be an asset.

Nerves, however, are a factor that can shake a player's confidence. If your nerves are not under control you become uncomfortable and fearful.

All good speakers, regardless of their experience, claim they are nervous before they speak. All good tennis players are nervous before a match. It gets the adrenaline flowing. After play begins experienced players usually are able to control their nervous tension. This should be your goal too.

When you become overly nervous you will probably change your style of play. You may start to hit tentatively and "push" the ball, or you may "over-hit" the ball and make errors. In either case you give your opponent an advantage.

There is not only an emotional reaction to nerves, there is also a physical reaction. You become tense. Your muscles tighten. Your strokes become short and jerky. All this means you make more errors. Occasionally a player will suffer an attack of leg cramps from nerves rather than from fatigue.

An antidote to a case of nerves is to slow down. Take more time between points. Relax. Don't rush. Take a deep breath before the start of each point. No matter how nervous you are, try not to show it. Act relaxed and confident and your case of nerves may disappear. Remember, if you look calm to your opponent, you might feel more calm yourself.

It's important to realize that no one is completely immune to nervousness. Everyone suffers an attack of nerves at some time. When you recognize this as a fact of life you can then face the problem of nerves and begin to control them.

The more important the match is to you, the greater your level of anxiety. Playing tennis may produce anxiety because you feel your reputation as a tennis player is on the line—and subconsciously you may think your reputation as a person is too. The more concerned you are about how you look playing, the greater the chance you will be overly anxious.

In order to play winning tennis you have to control your anxiety. Anxiety causes tension. Tension causes tense muscles. Tense muscles cause jerky shots. Jerky shots cause errors. Errors cause you to lose.

Coping Techniques

The antidote to stress and anxiety is *relaxation*. Learn to relax.

There is more than one way to relax. Learn different relaxation techniques, so you can switch to the one that best meets your needs at the particular time. There are many books available on the subject of relaxation. They have suggestions that can be easily adapted to use on the tennis court.

It's almost impossible to concentrate every second during a match. Concentrate during play and *relax between points*. Walk slowly and breathe deeply. Continue to relax until the ball is put in play. Do not start concentrating until you are about to serve or your opponent is about to serve, allow yourself the mental break. Regardless of how good your physical condition is, it still helps to relax between points.

Establish rituals between points to help maintain a relaxed

state in between playing. Try some "mini-relaxations" when you change sides. Sit down, take a few deep breaths, and just relax. Deep breathing helps lower pulse rate. However, remember that no matter how far you feel you have your opponent in the hole, you can't afford to relax *during the play*.

ANGER

You never help yourself, or your game, by getting angry. When you get mad at your opponent—or yourself—you lose your concentration and begin to make mistakes. The better you control your emotions, the better you can control the ball.

If you get a bad call, all it can cost you is one point. It's your reaction to the bad call that can cost you the match.

Don't react emotionally to bad calls—or bad breaks—they have a way of averaging out. So forget them. Optimism and confidence can help you fight off the adverse effect of a bad call or a bad shot.

If there are unforeseen delays — and there will be — it's counterproductive to get upset. Take time to practice some relaxation techniques or visualization. Use the time to your advantage, not your opponent's. If you allow yourself to get overly tense or angry, you are using the time to your opponent's advantage.

In addition to the emotions that are triggered on court by bad calls, good shots, mistakes, etc., there are emotions caused by off-court personal problems. It's difficult to wipe these out of your mind when you are playing, but this should be your goal. The more successful you are in doing this, the better you will be able to play. We will later look at some suggestions for keeping your concentration focused on the game in spite of mental and physical distractions.

The emotional downfall of most players is mistakes. Many players will get so upset over one simple mistake that they will make other mistakes. Often these secondary mistakes are more serious than the first one and cost the game. If you want to play winning tennis, put the mistake(s) out of your mind and get on with the game.

Out of control emotions will cause you to make unforced errors. In addition, your display of temper makes you look like a jerk. Why advertise it by getting mad? Control your temper. Allowing your temper to get the best of you shows your opponent that he/she has gotten the best of you. Remember to always seem in control, as this is a mental advantage over your opponent. You will be surprised how calm you can become if you just *act* calm.

FEAR

Everyone suffers fear at some time. Learn to harness your fear.

There is fear of playing someone better than you. There is fear of losing to someone ranked below you. There is fear that you won't look good when you play. There is fear of what other players and spectators will say about you.

Fear will do more to destroy your game or keep it from improving than any other thing. Overcome your fear by facing up to it. To paraphrase Franklin D. Roosevelt: the only thing you have to fear is fear itself. There is really nothing to be afraid of in tennis. The worst that could happen is that you lose the point, game, match, or tournament. But remember, tennis is not a life or death situation. It is only a game.

EMOTIONAL CONTROL

You should learn to harness your emotions to use when they can help you and block them out when they hinder you. Positive emotions can give you an extra burst of energy and confidence.

In tennis, as in everything else, you can't be competitive if you're not "raring to go" every time you play. This is the positive way to use your emotions.

When you have your emotions under control, you will be able to play better, but this does not guarantee that you will play a good game every day. Everyone has off days, even professional tennis players.

Also, remember that you are not the only one with emotions. Your opponent also has emotions. I cannot stress enough the importance of controlling your own emotions and your response to the emotional behavior of your opponent.

When your opponent displays his emotions, use them to learn his present mental state, but do not let them affect you. Whether he is angry, frustrated, disappointed, upset, happy, or expressing some other emotion, you can be sure the emotion will have some effect on his game. Learn to observe your opponent's mental state and capitalize on this information. For example, if he is frustrated, slow down the game to frustrate him more.

SELF-TALK

If you pay attention to what is going on in your mind when you play tennis (or do anything else), you will notice that you are having an almost constant running conversation with yourself.

"Wow, that was a great shot; she's really good! I know I couldn't have returned that ball!. . ." or "This guy sure is making a lot of mistakes; this should be a piece of cake!"

This internal "conversation" is called self-talk for the obvious reasons. It is important that you control what you say to yourself in self-talk. This talk has tremendous impact on you and your outlook on the situation at hand; in this case, the tennis game.

Self-talk can be good when it's positive and encouraging. Unfortunately, most self-talk is negative. Criticizing yourself when you make an error encourages less coordination between your mind and your body. It is important to "accentuate the positive and eliminate the negative" when it comes to self-talk.

It's easy to believe self-talk when it's negative. "I'm going to lose" becomes a self-fulfilling prophecy. Concentrate on positive self-talk. Say "I'm going to win." Do not allow negative thoughts to dominate your mind.

Develop a positive self-talk vocabulary so that your thought habits will become ones that will make you a winner instead of a loser. Replace the word *try* with *will*. This is more than a matter of semantics. It will establish a new attitude of dwelling on things you *will* do, rather than things you are just going to *try* to do. Habits begin as simple thoughts, like flimsy cobwebs. Then, with practice, they become unbreakable cables that shackle or strengthen your life.

Replace the word *can't* with *can* in your self-talk. Winners say, "Of course I can do this; I've practiced it mentally a thousand times." Losers say, "I can't possibly do this! It's too hard and I don't know how."

Become a *can* instead of a *can't* player, a winner instead of a loser. Remember, how you think and act affects your confidence and your confidence level affects how you play. Think and act like a winner and you will begin to play winning tennis.

CONFIDENCE

Tennis is a game of confidence. To a certain extent, confidence is the result of past successes; it comes from winning. If you start to lose, your confidence is likely to crumble. It is important to always believe that you can win, even when you are behind. This will enable you to maintain concentration and to play your best. Remember, when it comes to "crunch" time, a major key to winning is confidence.

You Have to Believe You Can Win The old saying, "Nothing succeeds like success" becomes "Nothing wins like winning" when applied to tennis. If you become a consistent winner, you will develop the mental advantage of self-confidence. Equally important, or perhaps more important, is the lack of confidence that is created in your opponent.

It helps to have friends to tell you that you can defeat a certain opponent, but that is not enough. *You* have to *really believe* that you can. You have to have the confidence that you can— and will—win.

Often the difference between the winner and the loser is the winner's self-confidence. If you go into a match believing you are going to lose, you probably will. Your lack of self-confidence becomes self-defeating.

The way to gain confidence is to recognize your weaknesses and practice hard to eliminate them. This develops the confidence that calms the "jitters."

Don't worry about hitting the ball hard, just return it safely. This will build your confidence and destroy your opponent's confidence.

The confident player expects to get his first serve in, hit perfect forehand and backhand shots, and put away overheads, and he is not rattled when he makes a mistake.

Worry Erodes Confidence We touched on this earlier, but I do not think it can be over-emphasized. You must not allow yourself to worry. If you start to worry about what your opponent is going to do, or whether or not you can win, it erodes your confidence and leads to errors.

When you are winning, your confidence is high. If you win the first set, your chances of winning the match are almost 90 percent. Knowing this, your confidence should be strengthened.

If you start to lose a few points there is the danger that your confidence will evaporate. Don't let this happen. Play with a certain margin of safety, but don't be overly cautious. When you play strongly and safely, your confidence will return. The pressure will again be on your opponent, leading him to make the errors.

Over-Confidence If two players are close in ability and one has two or three victories over the other, she develops more confidence. This confidence can often give her a psychological edge that enables her to continue to win. However, she should be careful not to become over-confident.

Remember the newspaper headline that read, "Dewey Defeats Truman"? Confidence is good, but be sure not to become so confident you fail to do your best—or underrate a Truman-like opponent. If you do, you may lose the "election" although you were assumed the winner.

MOTIVATION

Motivation is an important part of winning tennis games. You have to *want* to win. Self-motivation pushes you to train, practice, and become mentally tough. Self-motivation comes from within.

Not every tennis player is motivated to achieve the same thing. One type is motivated to win. Whatever he does, he thinks about winning and strives to win—and he usually does. The other type of player is concerned about losing. Whatever he does, his thoughts are focused on losing—and he usually does.

Be sure your motivation is the right kind—positive and strong. This is the motivation that wins.

CONCENTRATION

Concentrate *before* you start to play, and continue from the instant you step onto the court to focus all your attention on the game. Concentration is the antidote to most of the problems and distractions you face on the tennis court. Let tennis and only tennis occupy your mind. Never let your mind wander.

Seldom will you be able to play a match without being distracted, but the key to winning is to bring your concentration back to the game as quickly as possible.

Concentrate on what you are doing *now*. Play one point at a time. The previous shot—won or lost—is over. The next point hasn't been played yet. The one that counts is the one you are playing *now*. Playing winning tennis requires focus. While this is hard work, it is also fun. Don't be hard on yourself as you practice concentration, just notice when your mind is wandering and bring your attention back to the game. Practicing concentration should ease your existing tension, not create more.

Concentration in a match is focusing on the *present*, not thinking about the past or the future. Keeping your eyes on your racket strings, the ground, or the ball will help focus your attention between points. In addition, remember to breathe deeply and practice relaxation techniques.

Concentration will help you become more consistent and accurate. It is one of the best answers to the "junk ball"—that ball that keeps coming back and coming back. Remember to keep the ball in play. If your opponent is trying to do the same thing, outwait him. Concentration will help you do this.

Special Concerns

Outside distractions. Events beyond those happening on the tennis court can have a negative effect on your game. The events in your life off the court can distract you, as can activity and noise. The key to concentration is to block out anything going on in your private life or around you on the court that interferes with the tennis game you are playing. Concentrate on watching the ball and hit it where you planned to hit it, no matter where your opponent is.

Easy shots. It is even more important to concentrate on the easy shot than on the difficult shot. You are more likely to lose your concentration on the easy shot than on the difficult shot.

Fatigue. It's harder to maintain your concentration when you are tired. This is the time to force yourself to concentrate, especially when you are behind.

Uncertainty. Being sure of your strategy removes uncertainty. Having a game plan and staying with it is one of the best ways to maintain your concentration.

Excessive relief after a rally. The point after a long rally is *not* the time to relax. There is a tendency on the part of both players to let their concentration falter after a long rally. If you concentrate at this time and make a good shot or two, the odds are you will win the point.

Tension after an error. When you over-hit or make a sloppy error that you do not ordinarily make, it is usually because you failed to give the game your total concentration. Do not dwell on the mistake; regain your concentration and go forward.

Impatience. No matter what the level of your game, you must be patient and play one point at a time. The object is to win, not to play a fast, short match. Be patient. If you try to hit winners prematurely, you will make a lot of unforced errors. You must be patient. Don't lose baseline rallies by losing your patience and hitting the ball too hard.

If you miss a lot of shots early in the match, it is doubly important that you stay calm and patient. Be endlessly patient if your opponent is "out-steadying" you. Patience is hard to maintain if you become angry or full of worry. Remember to take deep breaths and relax. Frustration is not going to help you win the game.

Be especially patient when playing under windy conditions or on a clay court (because clay slows down the ball).

Frustration. Don't start talking to yourself during play. Don't yell at yourself, "Concentrate!" This is *not* concentration and will only make you more frustrated. If you want to get your concentration back, take a deep breath and get on with the game.

Big points. Obviously, the ideal is to maintain your concentration 100 percent of the time. Unfortunately, this is difficult if not impossible — even for the professional tennis player. Concentrate as much as you can, but bring extra concentration to bear on big points (such as set and match points).

DETERMINATION

Determination is the willingness to do those things that all winners do to maintain control of their matches combined with the resolve never to give up. Determination creates a winning mental attitude.

There are many factors that determine the winner in a match between players of equal ability. These factors include: momentum, psychology, fatigue, sun, wind, and luck. The most important factors, however, are concentration and determination to win.

Every game has crucial points where concentration, determination, and an all-out effort for only a brief period can mean the difference between winning and losing. It is impossible to put forth an all-out effort if you do not have determination. Some of the trouble spots for concentration are listed above. But concentration is not enough. It is sometimes easy to concentrate but not be determined enough to act.

Many players lose because they lack determination. They give up too easily—long before the match is over. They don't realize that if they just hang in there and concentrate, the tide may turn. Never, never quit until the last point has been played. You accomplish this by coupling determination with concentration.

Wanting to win is not enough. It takes concentration and determination. Many times the less skillful player wins, not simply because he wanted to win, but because he maintained his concentration and his determination to win.

As the concentration of an exhausted player drains away, he loses his determination and the possibility of defeat becomes probability. A player who has the determination to stick with it may eventually pass the player who has more ability and talent.

ANTICIPATION

Anticipation requires the awareness of two things; what your opponent *can* do and what he is *likely* to do in a given situation. Only when you are aware of these two things can you anticipate and react accordingly.

The secrets to good anticipation are concentration and alertness. Do not delay in getting away from the sideline and back to the center. Another significant aid in anticipation is to literally "be on your toes." The expression, "He got caught flat-footed," is, unfortunately, all too accurate a description of the tennis player.

Skillful anticipation will help you to start moving instantly *after* you hit the ball. While you are hitting the ball, concentrate only on the ball and where you are placing it. However, immediately after you have followed through with your racket, turn your concentration to your opponent. Watch her body and racket movement during her return stroke. Every player gives away the direction of her shot during the backswing.

Concentration helps you anticipate and prepare early so you can get to a lot of balls that running alone won't reach.

Eyes on the Ball One element contributing to successful anticipation is *keeping your eye on the ball*. When you begin looking at the ball the instant it leaves your opponent's racket, you can see immediately where it is going and how fast so you have a better chance to get in position to return it. Couple this with watching your opponent's backswing and you can stay one step ahead of him all the way. Concentration helps you do this.

If the ball is hit three feet over the net, it will probably land deep in your court. If the ball barely clears the net, it will probably land shallow in your court—unless it's hit unusually hard.

Practice Practice your concentration and anticipation when you are a spectator. Since you are not playing, this gives you an opportunity to devote your full attention to trying to determine the direction the player is going to hit the ball. Do this by observing the movement of the player's arms, body, and racket.

COMMITMENT

In order to become a consistent winner, you have to have concentration, determination, and confidence. Anticipation and commitment are the natural outgrowths of these.

Remember, lessons won't do it; practice won't do it; and playing won't do it. Oh, they will make you a better player, but not a consistent winner. To become a better player you must have commitment—and you must concentrate to maintain that commitment.

GAMESMANSHIP

There is a fine line between sportsmanship and gamesmanship. However, within the bounds of good sportsmanship, use gamesmanship at every opportunity. It's most effective when your opponent is not even aware of it.

Gamesmanship begins with knowing the temperamental make-up of your opponent. Is he highstrung? Easygoing? How does he react to tension? Does he lose his confidence easily?

Feinting Feinting to make your opponent think you are going to poach is a legitimate tactic in doubles. There are many other things you can do to upset your opponent that fall within the boundary of both sportsmanship and gamesmanship. Adhere to Colonel Nick Powell's book on the "Code" and you will not cross the line between the two. ("Code of Conduct" is available free of charge from the U.S.T.A to any member. A non-member will have to pay a small fee.)

Cheating is Calling a shot out that was clearly in is not gamesmanship. It is
Not cheating. When you do this or use other similar tactics, you are
Games- not crossing the line, you are jumping over it.
manship In the book of Mark, chapter 8, verse 36 we read, "For what shall it profit a man, if he shall gain the whole world, and lose his own soul?" This can be paraphrased to read, "For what shall it profit a player, if he wins the match, and loses the respect and friendship of his fellow players?"

Unfortunately, almost every tennis club or group of players has a cheater. He may cheat only when he needs a point. He may cheat by calling a good shot out. Or he may be a vocal cheat, a pantomime cheat, a bad sport cheat, a line cheat, or a combination cheat. How sad. Tennis is a game. Enjoy it, be competitive, but remember, it is just a game.

9

Practice

You often hear the expression, "I've paid my dues," used by a person to indicate that she started at the bottom and worked her way up. As a tennis player, you should look on your practice as "paying your dues." You have to begin at the bottom and work your way up if you are to become a winner.

The more you practice, the more you will improve and obviously, the more you improve, the more matches you will win. Few players perform anywhere near their potential, due in part to their lack of effective practice. Effective practice is extremely important for perfecting your game.

CONCENTRATE

Make sure that you bring the same intensity of concentration to the practice session that you bring to a match. Many club players treat practice sessions casually. This is a mistake. If you're going to make your practice sessions productive, you must approach them seriously. Practice with intensity.

If practice is to be productive, it cannot be done carelessly. Practice should be done with conscious effort to make changes and corrections. This chapter provides advice on how to practice most effectively.

HAVE SPECIFIC GOALS

Some players think practice consists just of hitting a tennis ball. Not so. You need to plan your workout carefully. Skill in tennis develops more quickly from systematic and planned practice than from merely hitting the ball at random.

Warmup   Remember to warm up before you begin an intense practice session. It's just as important to warm up before you practice as it is to warm up before you play a match. Start out slowly. Begin by hitting easy balls for a few minutes.

Use Good   Many players practice with old balls. You should practice with
Balls   balls that have the same degree of liveliness as the balls you will be using when you play a match. If you play with markedly inferior balls, you will begin to overhit when playing with good balls.

PRACTICE TO IMPROVE

While you cannot do anything to create natural ability—it is by definition innate — you can develop the ability you have by practice. Some individuals are blessed with more natural athletic ability than others, but unless they practice, they will be defeated by less talented players who do practice.

You can't learn to play the piano — or tennis — just by watching someone do it. You have to practice. No matter how much natural ability you have, you can't go from beginner to top flight player without practicing and going through the intermediate stages.

PRACTICE TO AVOID MISTAKES

Most players are defeated by the mistakes they make, not directly by their opponents. Often when two players are closely matched, mistakes and breaks are what make the difference. This was discussed in the chapter on the psychological aspects of tennis.

You will never improve if you continue to make the same mistakes over and over. Learn from your mistakes. Do what is necessary to correct them. You avoid mistakes by practice, practice, practice.

If you constantly make errors under pressure on your second serve or on one of your strokes, there is the temptation to blame it on nerves, tension, or choking. This may be true, but we have addressed how to handle those aspects of the mistake. Now you need to look at the mechanical deficiencies you bring to the game. Practice time is the time to develop the technical, mechanical aspects of your game.

PRACTICE ENSURES AUTOMATIC STROKE TECHNIQUE _____

Once you start playing a match, you should be able to hit by instinct and not worry about things like getting your racket back and stepping into the ball.

The solution is to practice until you have that particular stroke "grooved." You will know when you have a stroke "grooved" because it will come as second nature to you. You will not have to think about the mechanics of the shot; you will automatically execute it correctly and comfortably. If you practice the same shot three different ways, you will be hesitant before using it because you will have to choose one of the different ways to use. When practicing a shot, your first priority should be consistency. This helps the execution come naturally.

When you try to practice several strokes at once, you can't "groove" any of them, and you'll probably overlook something important. Don't try to learn all your strokes at the same time. Practice *one* stroke at a time.

If you have to think about turning sideways, getting the racket back, hitting the ball in front of your body, following through, etc., you won't have time to play tennis. The time to do this kind of thinking is when you practice. Practice creates muscle memory, which lets you do the mechanical things automatically.

Practice for perfection. Work on winning shots. If you don't try a shot in practice, you'll have difficulty hitting it in a match. You will be more familiar with, and therefore more comfortable with, shots you have practiced.

PRACTICE GOOD HABITS _____

One especially good way to improve your game is to seek out your weaknesses and practice to correct them. When you work on your weaknesses, be sure you don't neglect your strengths. Be sure to practice your strongest shots as well.

There are only two things you can practice: bad habits and good habits. If all you do is practice bad habits, you'll get worse instead of better. When you practice, be sure you are practicing good habits. This is one important reason to get professional advice and lessons.

You will make more winning shots if you practice with definite targets. Working on placements this way will build up your percentage of winning shots. Practice is the time to work on your game's kinks, the trouble spots. If you hear yourself saying, "I *always* miss that shot!" that's the time to learn the correct way to make the shot. Ask a professional, or a friend who consistently makes the shot you are having difficulty making. This is the "how to do it" part of playing.

LENGTH OF PRACTICE

A half-hour to an hour of good hard practice is better than two or three hours of haphazard hitting. The length of time you practice doesn't determine how much you improve your game.

You have to enjoy playing tennis to play winning tennis and you also have to enjoy practicing to improve your game. A practice session should be fun. If you are simply forcing yourself to practice, you will not benefit from it.

As soon as your enthusiasm wanes during practice, stop. You can practice too much, but only if you don't really want to practice or you are not in good physical condition.

Practice without enthusiasm is wasted effort and is often the practice of bad habits—mental and physical.

CROSSCOURT SHOTS

There are three reasons to practice crosscourt shots. First, the net is six inches lower in the middle. Second, the crosscourt distance is greater. Third, crosscourt shots tend to force your opponent off the court so he is more likely to be out of position for his return and less likely to be able to get back in position for your return.

Spend time practicing shots to the corners; this is the way to run your opponent and also hit winners. Practice these shots from different court positions, using your backhand and forehand. You should be familiar with the exact amount of force required to reach the corners from any spot on the court.

DON'T FORGET YOUR SERVE

Many players spend most of their practice time rallying and spend very little time practicing their serve. This is a mistake. Spend some extra time on your serve, and your game will improve dramatically. Practice especially the placement of the serve, including depth. Remember, there is no excuse for not practicing your serve. You don't even need a practice partner.

First work on developing a *dependable second serve*, then work on adding velocity to it to convert it into "first serve" quality.

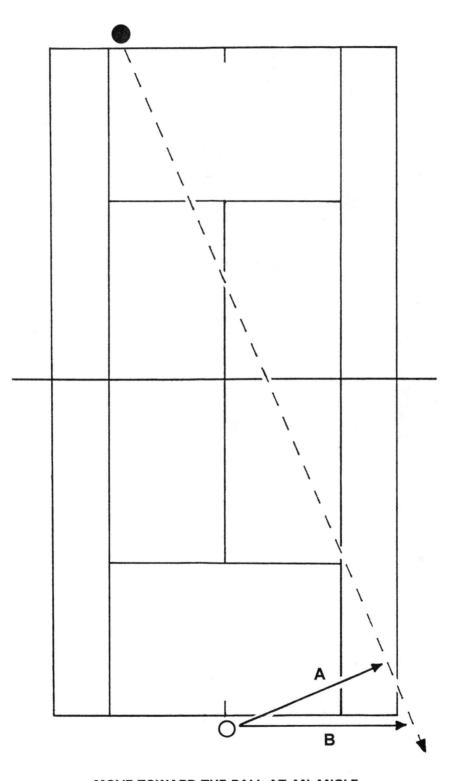

MOVE TOWARD THE BALL AT AN ANGLE
When the ball is hit crosscourt, don't run to it parallel to the base line (B). Run to the ball at a right angle to its flight (A). This will "cut it off at the pass."

Carlotta Browder, 68, fires off an overhand serve as she practices her tennis game for the Senior Olympics. Courtesy The Charlotte Observer.

Practice Your Service Toss When you think of practice, you think of hitting balls on a tennis court; but courts, practice partners, and time to practice are not always available. There is, however, a part of your game that can be practiced anywhere and anytime. That's your service toss. Practice your service toss. All you need is a ball.

SPEED DRILLS

Practice is more than just hitting tennis balls. If you want to improve your strength, add some speed to your practice drills to emphasize explosiveness. Remember, explosiveness is relative; older players should never make these exercises too explosive. Work on the drills gradually and do them only once or twice a week.

BACKBOARD PRACTICE

If a wall or backboard is available, use it to groove your strokes. The backboard will return your ball every time so you can im prove your strokes and get a lot of practice done in a short time. When you go on the court to hit against a practice partner, you'll only have to adjust your timing, not the mechanics of the stroke.

MIRROR PRACTICE

Practicing your strokes in front of a full-length mirror (without a ball, of course) will help you groove them. You may feel self-conscious the first time you try this, but it is a very effective way of seeing what you are doing correctly (and/or incorrectly).

MATCH TIME IS NOT PRACTICE TIME

Once you are playing a match you are not on court to practice, but to win. Although you may learn while playing a match, this is not practice time.

Too many club players are satisfied with practicing *as they play competitively* rather than before. If you want to see dramatic improvement in your game, you must practice. Repetition is essential to learning tennis, so practice your strokes over and over until they become second nature.

PRACTICE AND PRACTICE SETS

Most players want to play sets when they practice, because part of the fun of tennis is seeing if you're better than your opponent. But you will experience the thrill of winning more often if you devote most of your practice time to grooving your strokes.

This doesn't mean you should never play practice sets. There is a big difference in hitting during a practice rally when you are under no stress or pressure and hitting during a match. It's important that you also play some practice sets so you can become "match tough" and (eventually) "tournament tough."

When you are playing practice sets, try allowing yourself only one serve on each point. Since you must get every serve in, you will develop a safer serve—one with not as much pace, but with greater consistency. By doing this you will gain confidence in your serve and not have to fear double faults.

PRACTICE PARTNERS

If possible, you should vary your practice partners. It is very important that you practice against different types of players—

retrievers, hard hitters, spin artists, net rushers, big servers, etc. Each type of practice partner provides a different challenge that can prepare you to play different types of players.

When you are working on a particular stroke or trying to change your style of play, you should practice against a weaker player. If you play someone who is your equal or better, you will be pressed on your strokes and thus not be able to concentrate on skill development.

MAGIC WON'T DO IT

Fred Klein of *The Wall Street Journal* wrote jokingly in his sport column, "A belief in magic is characteristic of primitive societies and tennis players." How true. We expect some gimmick or gadget to suddenly turn us into winning tennis players without paying the price of practice. It never happens that way. Your practice — not some magical gimmick—will determine whether you become a winning tennis player.

There is no substitute for hitting tennis balls. It's not practice that makes perfect, it's perfect practice that makes perfect —or at least improves your game.

10

Position

Your location and movement on the tennis court will affect your game and may well determine whether you win or lose. If you are not in the correct position to return the ball, you will be unable to play winning tennis. It is your movement that enables you to get to the ball so you can return it effectively.

Watch the ball is probably the advice given most often to tennis players. A big secret of always being in position is to watch the ball. Always watch the ball instead of looking in the direction you intend to hit the ball.

You as a player have to get to the ball, get in proper position to hit the ball, and then hit it with the correct stroke. Watching the ball helps you do all of these things. If you don't "keep your eye" on the ball, you will never become a winning tennis player, but you have to be able to reach it once you see where it is going.

It is important to watch both the ball and the backswing of your opponent in order to better anticipate the direction of the ball being returned. Many think they anticipate better than they do and they often make the mistake of substituting guesswork for anticipation. They try to *guess* where their opponent is going to hit the ball and move too soon, thus opening the court and allowing their opponents to take advantage of the premature move. Avoid the temptation to use blind anticipation.

Being ready to move promptly in order to maintain correct court position allows you to reach the ball much sooner without actually moving *before* you know the direction of the return. This alert readiness eliminates the need to guess where your opponent is going to hit the ball. You will feel more confident about making it to the ball if you are confident in your ability to move quickly in any direction.

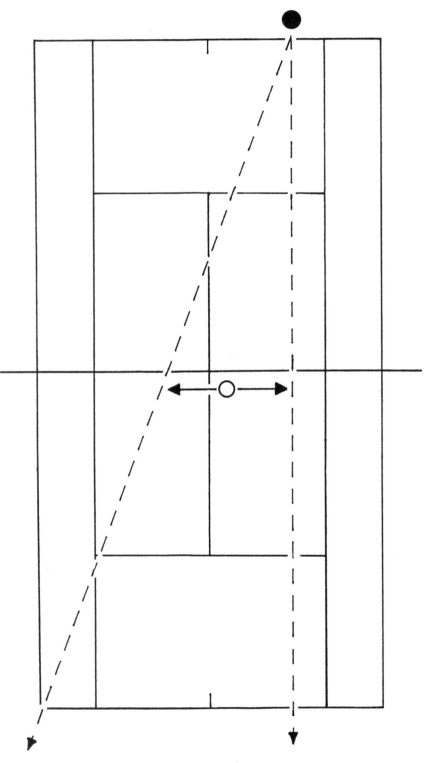

POSITION AT NET

When you have hit an approach shot and moved to the net, position yourself in the center of possible returns. This will give you the best chance to cut off passing shots both down the line and crosscourt.

COURT POSITION

Court position is even more important for returning than is anticipation. Where you stand while you wait for your opponent's return can mean the difference between getting to the ball or not.

The court position you select in the instant after you return the ball may determine whether you win or lose that point. Start moving immediately after you hit the ball. Don't wait to see where your ball lands. Get back in position.

If you stop and stay in the position from which you hit your approach shot, you will be late getting to the net. If you don't know where the ball will be returned, you should be in a position that allows you to access all portions of the court quickly.

Select a "home base" to which you naturally return when there is any doubt about where your opponent is going to hit the ball. Otherwise, position yourself so you will be in the "center of possible returns."

Home Base There are only two positions on a tennis court at any given time —where you are and where your opponent is. Not where you were or where you ought to be. Just where you are. Your present position, right or wrong, and your opponent's position determine where you should hit the ball.

BASELINE When playing from the baseline, always move toward the cen-
HOME BASE ter immediately after you hit the ball—even if you are only a step or two away from it. Normally, your "home base" position should be about three feet behind the center of the baseline.

NET HOME Your second, or "advanced base," position should be about six
BASE to twelve feet from the net. When you are at the net, always cover the center of possible returns. This means your position should be equally far from the sideline (on the side of the court where you hit your approach shot) and the point where a crosscourt shot would cross the net and still be in. This will put you in the best position to reach both a down-the-line return and a crosscourt return.

Special *Spin.* Be especially alert when your opponent hits a ball with a
Concerns lot of spin. This spin will affect the bounce, depending on the type of spin put on the ball. The ball may bounce into your body, break away from you, or bounce high or low.

Drop shots. If your return will hit near the baseline, the chances are your opponent's return will be more shallow than usual. In that case, you may want to move forward while your shot is still in the air. The shot return may give you a chance to "put it away." When you are playing an opponent who frequently hits drop shots, play in just a little, even if this means you have to hit an occasional ball in the air from the backcourt.

Overhead returns. Most overhead errors are caused by failure to move back far enough before hitting the ball. Try for a position where the ball would drop onto your chest if you didn't hit it.

Deep shots. When your opponent hits a deep shot to you, it's important that you make every effort to make your return a deep shot so your opponent will not have a short ball he can "put away."

MOVEMENT

Knowing good position will not help you if you are not able to move from your current position into the best possible position for the return. Movement on a tennis court is different from any other movement to which you are accustomed. Tennis distances are so short and time so limited that anticipation and a quick start are essential. In order to handle the movement required of you, you must have quick feet.

FOOTWORK

Running on a tennis court is very different from running in a track meet. While going to the net is forward running similar to traditional running, this movement requires sudden stops and frequent changes in direction. The tennis player who runs forward must be prepared for all of this and be able to quickly move again.

It doesn't matter if you have perfect strokes, if you don't get to the ball you can't hit it. Even if you do get to the ball you may plant your feet too late or in the wrong position. Good footwork will enable you to get to the ball and have time to hit it with an unhurried swing.

Good footwork means speed in reaching the ball and balance when hitting the ball. Footwork is the foundation of your movement on the court. If your feet don't carry you to the correct position to execute your stroke, you will probably make an error or hit a weak return.

On the move.

Don't Plant   Planting is for gardening, not tennis. Don't plant your feet too
Your Feet   soon and wait for the ball to come to you. Those who have seen
Ken Rosewall play have noticed that he keeps shuffling his feet
—sometimes only an inch or two—until he is in perfect position to hit the ball.

Never stand and admire a shot you have just made that you
think is a winner. If you do, you will often see your opponent
hit your "impossible-to-return" shot, and you will find yourself
out of position. Get back in position immediately.

It's important to move into position as quickly as possible
so you will not be rushed when stroking the ball. When you are
late getting into position you will have to hurry the execution of
the stroke, which will increase the chance of making an error.

Keep moving your feet so that if you misjudge the bounce or
where the ball will land, you are not committed. This movement
will allow you to take an extra step toward or away from the ball
as necessary. It also will enable you to hit the ball from your
comfortable hitting zone. Moving your feet is the only way you
can move into the correct position to stroke the ball when you
have misjudged it.

Speed and Balance
There is more to good footwork than just running to the ball. The secret of good footwork is a *quick* start. The secret to a quick start is being on your toes, hopping or bouncing, ready to move as soon as your opponent hits the ball. If you wait flat-footed you will be left "at the gate."

Much of the movement on a tennis court is side to side and much of this is side-skipping, since the first skip is a push-off that enables you to start quickly. To improve your quickness in changing directions, be "bouncy" on your toes and practice pushing off with your left foot to move to the right and with your right foot to move to the left.

While side-to-side speed and forward-and-back speed are both important, side-to-side speed is more essential to winning. More players hit wide shots that move you from side to side than hit shots that bring you up and then drive you back. When you are on the baseline and need to move only six or seven feet to the right or left, skip sideways—if your opponent has not hit the ball too hard.

Footwork and Injury
Sloppy footwork *can* be caused by fatigue, but it is more often the result of laziness. You take one long step and stretch for the ball, instead of taking two shorter steps that would put you in proper position to hit the ball without stretching. If you want to win, don't be lazy. Don't economize on footwork. It's that extra step —or half step—that can get you in position to hit a good shot.

Tennis players suffer injuries to almost every part of the body. One of the most common injuries is disabling pain in the lower back and down one leg. This is usually brought on by awkward stretching—often the result of a player not taking that extra step and having to stretch out to hit the ball. This is typical of how players acquire a slipped (prolapsed) intervertebral disk.

To avoid such injury, it is important to learn to move properly toward the ball. Let your feet and legs do the moving for you. If you do this you will not have to bend or stretch awkwardly to hit the ball, and your body is more likely to remain upright.

Hop, Skip, and Bounce
If you keep your feet in almost continuous motion with short little hops or at least weave your body from side to side—especially when waiting to receive serve—you will be able to start more quickly to meet the ball.

Good players are always moving with a hop, skip, bounce, or shift. Emulate them. If you are always moving when the ball is in play, you will be able to get to balls that the player who is standing still just can't reach.

Moving sideways after return, eyes still on the ball.

If you stand still physically you are probably not mentally alert—and vice versa. Keeping on the move physically will help you stay mentally alert. Remember to concentrate; stay alert even if you think your opponent cannot return your shot. Usually, getting caught "flat-footed" is the result of failing to expect your opponent to return the ball. Always be prepared to return the ball until it is actually out of play.

Practice Your Footwork Footwork can be practiced without a racket and ball or even a tennis court. Use your imagination and pretend you are moving to get in position to hit a ball—forward and backward or sideways. Make it a form of practice with visualization.

Footwork and the Eyes When a player's footwork begins to slow down, the usual explanation given is slowing reflexes and age. While this may be true, there may be another reason that is overlooked. That is the "eye-foot" coordination. When the eyes begin to fail, the ball isn't seen as quickly or as well, so the message to the brain to start the footwork is slow in being relayed to the feet—thus a slow start. If your own footwork is slowing down, consider the possibility that at least a part of the reason may be your eyes. You may need glasses.

11

Serve and Service Return

The serve is the single most important stroke in tennis. A good, strong, well-placed serve is an asset for the server. A poor, weak serve is an asset for the receiver.

The serve is the one stroke you have complete control over. You don't have to guess where to stand. You don't have to run to get to the ball. Make the most of it. You and you alone decide when, where, and how fast you will serve.

When you get your first serve in, hitting the ball deep with good placement, you put pressure on your opponent and there isn't much he can do that will hurt you.

SPIN FOR SERVE

The winner of the spin for serve is in a position to make a choice that could affect the outcome of the match.

Beginning players are often not aware of the importance of the spin for serve and the choices available. The player who wins the spin has four choices. These are:
- he can choose to serve
- he can choose to receive
- he can choose the side
- he can have his opponent choose first

Most players, when they win the spin, automatically choose to serve. Some, however, will choose to receive instead of serve. This is a good choice if you do not feel properly warmed up as it gives you some additional warmup time before you have to serve. In addition, it may give you a slight psychological advantage because your opponent will expect you to choose to serve and/or may not be warmed up himself.

You may defer the first choice to your opponent. This is a good tactic if you are concerned about being on a specific end

Note position and toss.

of the court for your first serve. You might have to wait until the second game if your opponent opts to serve first, but you will be in the position of your choice, nonetheless.

PRACTICE YOUR SERVE

One of the most difficult things to understand about the average tennis player is why he can't serve any better than he does. He doesn't have to run for the ball when he serves. He can hit it from the same location, the same stance, the same distance from the net, and with the ball in the same place in the air.

If that player is *you*, do something about it. You can practice your serve alone and at your convenience. Why not start today to improve your serve?

SERVICE TOSS

The toss is probably the most underrated part of the serve. Without a good, accurate, consistent toss, there is no way you will be able to hit a good, accurate, consistent serve. It will help you to make a better toss if you hold only one ball in your hand.

Different types of serves demand a toss to different locations. In order to be consistent in your serve, you must consistently toss the ball to the particular location desired for the type of serve you are hitting. This is one of the major reasons you must control your toss.

If your serve varies from day to day, the first thing to consider is your toss. Begin to notice if it varies from day to day. It may be too high, or too low, or too far in front of you, or too far back of you, or too far to the side. Make sure that you are consistent with your toss, you will be amazed at the improvement in your serve.

As you get older, the serve is one of the first parts of your game to go. This is an additional reason the service toss and timing are so important.

SERVICE ROUTINE

Don't stall, but do take your time in getting ready to serve. Establish a service routine and rhythm. It's a good habit to bounce the ball a certain number of times before you serve. By doing this you can be sure your opponent is ready, but of even more importance is the calming effect this has on you. Even a short service routine allows you to take a deep breath and gather your concentration before serving. This calming effect gives you a chance to take a deep breath before serving. Be prepared. Think *where* and *how* you want to serve.

Position If you have a service routine, don't dramatically vary where you stand for different placements. If you do, your position can tip off your opponent to the placement of your serve. To avoid giving him this advantage, move *only slightly* if you do vary from your usual position. The average receiver won't notice this small change in serving position, but it will give you a better serving angle.

PLACEMENT

The percentage serve is down the center of the court, since this does not create an angle for the receiver's return. A good rule when you are serving in the deuce court is to place eighty percent down the middle. In the ad court, go for fifty percent down the middle. Vary your serve and serve wide occasionally to keep your opponent guessing and off balance.

When you are serving don't overlook hitting directly at the receiver. This is called a "jam serve" and can be very effective.

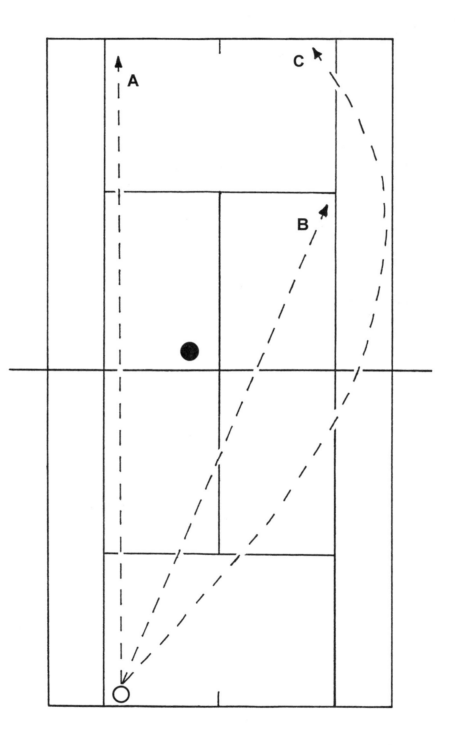

PLAYING AGAINST NET MAN

When your opponent has hit a good approach shot and moved to the net,
you have three options: (1) hit down the line to A, (2) hit crosscourt to B, or
(3) lob to C.

It will often force a weak return simply because it is difficult for the receiver to move to the side quickly enough to return it strongly.

FIRST SERVE

You have an immediate psychological advantage over your opponent when you get your first serve in. This creates extra pressure on the receiver to return the first serve, even if it isn't a hard serve. The receiver always expects the first serve to be tougher than the second serve and this anticipation often causes him to make an error or to hit a poor return. If the first serve is a fault, the receiver relaxes and can usually make a good return on the second serve.

If you are serving the tenth game in a match with a 4-5 score, it is imperative that your first serve is good. If it isn't, your second serve will give your opponent a chance to attack and put the pressure on you and perhaps get a service break that will give him the set.

Your serving goal should be to get at least seventy percent of your first serves in. On those days when your first serve has "gone out to lunch" and is good less than fifty percent of the time—you have a problem. Replace your first serve with your second serve until you can get your serve "grooved" again and you are more comfortable. Take your time. Don't rush your serve.

Aces The average player observes the pro hitting the traditional hard first serve. Since he wants to play like a pro, he tries the same procedure. Unfortunately, when he blasts his first serve, it often goes into the net or hits the backstop, then his second serve is merely "tapped" in—just begging to be put away. If you're not a pro, you can't play like a pro. Don't try to.

You will be able to serve more aces with *reasonable speed and placement* than by hitting "cannonball" serves that are seldom good. An occasional first service ace will not be much of an asset if most of your first serves are faults.

Get Your First Serve Over the Net Most players know how important it is to get their first serve in. What many don't realize is how important it is to get the first serve *over the net*—even though the serve may be long. (More first serves are hit into the net than are hit long.)

If your first serve hits the net, the receiver can relax immediately. However, if the serve clears the net, the receiver continues to be under pressure until the ball actually hits the surface of the court—even if the ball is long. This added pressure can be an important factor in creating additional tension on your opponent.

SECOND SERVE

You are only as good as your second serve. Nothing will improve your game more than depth and accuracy on the second serve.

Do not rush your second serve. Many players hurry back to the baseline after missing the first serve and immediately toss the ball up for a second serve—and immediately serve a double fault. If the first serve is a fault, take time to relax. Decide what you need to do, concentrate, and then serve. Take even more time on your second serve before important points.

There's always an element of fear involved when you are about to hit your second serve. The pressure is even greater on important points. You know you must get it in or you'll lose the point. If you do not consciously relax, your muscles tend to respond to anxiety by contracting. This increases the probability that you will either serve a fault or just "pitty-pat" the ball across the net.

The second serve is often more important than the first serve. If the second serve isn't good, you have served a double fault and have lost the point. A "powder puff" second serve is almost the same as no second serve. It is an invitation to the receiver to put it away or at least to put you on the defensive.

The average player is better off having two *consistent second serves* than a hard first serve that rarely goes in. A well-placed, medium-paced spin serve that goes in is better than a hard serve that is a fault.

Hitting a good second serve poses a problem for professional players as well as for the average club player. On more than one occasion I have seen some of the top ranked pros serve a double fault on game or even match point. Jack Kramer, the best exponent of the "big serve," once said, "The second serve is the shot that made or broke more players than any other." Enough said.

Double Faults The most important factor in a second serve is to make it go in. Don't give away free points by serving double faults. Double faults not only lose points, but psychologically discourage the server and encourage the receiver.

When you serve more double faults than aces, your serve is not an asset, it's a liability.

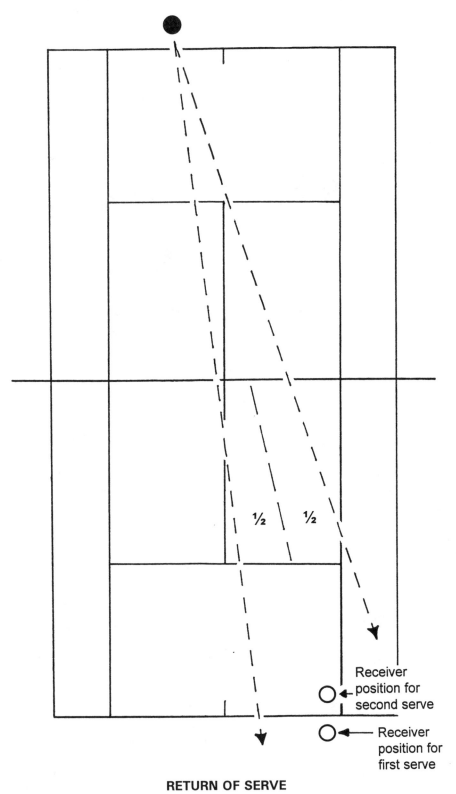

RETURN OF SERVE

When receiving serve, position yourself in the center of possible serves.

SERVICE RETURN

The service return is the second most important stroke in tennis. This is the shot that you must hit on (nearly) half the points you play if you want the point to continue.

When receiving the serve, *keep your eyes on the ball* from the time your opponent tosses it into the air until it lands in your court and you hit it.

You have five shots to choose from when you return a serve. These are (1) drive, (2) chip, (3) block, (4) lob, and (5) drop. Which of these you use will depend on (1) how hard the serve is hit, (2) the placement of the serve, (3) what the server does after hitting the serve, and (4) your own ability to execute the shot you select. (These terms are defined in the glossary for the beginner.)

If you have scouted your opponent and know how he is apt to respond to particular shots, this information will aid you in deciding which shots to use on the return of serve. For example, if the serve is not hit very hard and your opponent has trouble with drop shots, you may choose to use a drop shot. If the opponent rushes to the net immediately following his serve, you may choose to lob. I cannot tell you what shot to choose in every situation. Experience and observation will tell you this.

Waiting Position   There are a number of factors that determine your best position while waiting to receive serve. Where the server stands to serve, the type of spin he puts on his serve, and whether or not he is right or left-handed must all be considered. While there is no substitute for being on the court and observing your opponent, there are a few tips to remember that will help you be in a position close to your best choice before you have a feel for each particular server. The important thing is to get in the *center of possible serves*.

If the server stands close to the center mark, move toward the center of the court yourself. If he moves away from the center, position yourself a bit closer to the sideline.

Don't stand *on* the baseline to return a hard first serve. When you do this you may hit an *occasional* sensational return, but you will not have any consistent ability to return serve. If the goal is to play winning tennis, you must be able to return hard first serves consistently. You do this by standing far enough *behind* the baseline to give yourself time to see the serve and hit a good return.

Ready Stance Now that you know where you are standing, let's talk about how you stand as you wait. Most authorities suggest the typical athlete's stance — a crouched, ready, alert position with the weight forward on your toes. This position enables you, the receiver, to move more quickly in any direction.

Never stand still to receive serve. If you observe the top pros, you will notice that most of them take a little hop just as the server hits the ball. You may not be able to time this little hop but you can sway a little from side to side. The important thing is not to be caught "flat-footed." When you are already in motion, you have a better chance to get to the ball.

Placement If you can detect a pattern in your opponent's serve, try to decide *ahead of time* where and how you are going to return serve. Below are some broad guidelines that will help determine good returns for specific patterns.

- If the first serve is consistently good (within bounds) and hit to your forehand, return crosscourt.
- If the second serve is consistently weak, return with a drop shot.
- If the player follows his serve to the net, return down the middle of the court. No matter how good he volleys, he will find it difficult to produce an angle from the center of the court. In a situation like this you will almost always have a chance for another shot when you can try to pass him or lob.
- If the ball comes to your backhand, do not try to run around it to return it with your forehand. Only an excellent player who has a very strong forehand—or backhand—should run around a serve to hit it with his stronger stroke. Even then, the wisdom of such a move is questionable. This is not a maneuver for the average player.
- If your opponent serves wide to the deuce court it will often give you the chance to hit a down-the-line winner.
- When the server hits you a wide angle ball, run forward *and* sideways toward the ball. This cuts down on the angle, gets you to the ball quicker, and puts you in a better position to hit an outright winner than you would have if you had merely skipped sideways.

Deciding ahead of time where and how you will return serves won't work every time. It's better, however, to try to do some advance planning than to wait until the serve is in your court to decide what to do. The key to a successful return of serve is direction rather than speed.

Regardless of how and where you have decided to return serve, always keep your plan flexible so you can alter your response if necessary. It will not work to your advantage to return service with the same shot each time as your opponent will quickly learn what to expect. When you vary your service return—stroke and placement—you put pressure on the server.

Doubles In doubles you'll usually win or lose depending on your ability to break serve. To break serve you have to be able to return serve. There is more pressure on the receiver in doubles since there is already one opponent at the net ready to cut off the service return.

In doubles the safest return is crosscourt. This gives you the most court to hit in, the lowest part of the net to hit over, and keeps your return away from the net man. The second safest alternative return of serve in doubles is an offensive lob over the player who is at the net.

DRAWING A DOUBLE FAULT

If your opponent is one who hits a hard first serve, he may have trouble with his second serve. Often players with hard first serves have difficulty hitting a slower ball for the second serve because they rely heavily on their first serves. If this is the case, you may be able to draw a double fault by doing the following: Prepare to receive his first hard serve from a position *back* of the baseline, but if his first serve is a fault, immediately move a couple of feet *inside* the baseline. Then, at the moment the server is about to toss up the ball for his second serve he will look toward you. That is the time to let him see you inching forward—toward the service line.

You will be surprised how often doing this will cause the average player to hit his second serve into the net. One possible reason your opponent may make this type of error is because your moving closer to him may change his perspective of distance. Or perhaps it is the added pressure caused by seeing you take the initiative.

Sometimes even the pros fall for this maneuver. In the finals of the 1990 French Open young Michael Chang was playing Ivan Lendl. As I watched the match on TV, I was amazed to see Chang do exactly what I outlined above. On the second serve (match point), he moved up almost to the service line. And what happened? Lendl served a fault and Chang won the match.

12

Winning Shots and Percentage Tennis

There is no one right or wrong way to hit the ball. If you can keep the ball in play one more time than your opponent, how you do it is of secondary importance. There are, however, shots that have proved dependable over time and are likely to produce winners.

HITTING THE BALL

Forehand and backhand are the most frequently used shots in the game of tennis. Remember that different shots that are not used as often will also win points for you. The best players are the ones who can win points utilizing a variety of different shots. It is important to know which shot to use and when. Experiment and find the shots that work best for you.

Shorten Your Grip Although I know that this is not a "how to hold the racket" book, this is one tip that I want to include to benefit the beginning player. If you are finding it difficult to hit the ball accurately, try gripping the handle of the racket closer to the head.

The racket is an extension of your arm. The farther the head of the racket is from your hand, the more difficult it is to hit the ball accurately. If you don't believe me, try to hit a small object, such as a tennis ball, with a broom that you are holding by the end of the handle. Keep moving your hand up the handle of the broom toward the head and notice how much more accurate you become the closer you move toward the head. By the time your hand is next to the head of the broom, you can hit the ball almost every time.

If you have been having difficulty hitting the ball accurately, grip the handle closer to the head of your racket. You will find that your game will improve.

When to Hit the Ball

Have you ever been in a position to hit the ball, but you thought it was going out, or long, so you let it go—but it was good? Of course you have. We all have. Remember, if there is the slightest possibility that the ball may be in, *hit it back*. It's not worth taking the chance that it might be out or long and losing the point. In addition, every return you make successfully improves your confidence and undermines your opponent's confidence. Be in position to return every shot. If you are in position to return, you can more clearly see if the ball is in or not. If you assume it is out and do not prepare to return, by the time you see that the ball is good, it will be too late to effectively stay in the point. Always try to return every ball.

Hitting the Ball Long

It takes extra concentration to avoid hitting the ball long. When you run forward to reach the ball, the added momentum of your forward motion increases the velocity of the ball. In addition, the distance to your opponent's baseline is now shorter than it was when you were rallying from your backcourt. Thus, if you hit the ball with the same power you have been using, you will likely hit the ball long.

When you are rallying from the baseline and your opponent suddenly hits the ball short, this poses both opportunity and hazard. The opportunity is presented for you to hit an approach shot and go to the net. The hazard is that you may hit the ball long. When you have to run forward to reach a short ball, be careful how you hit it. Concentrate and take a little pace off your stroke.

DROP SHOT

The drop shot is one of the most underused shots in tennis. Drop shots are especially effective against players who can't move quickly.

The drop shot is not a shot for every player. It can, however, give you an advantage if you execute it properly and use it at the appropriate time. Practice enables you to do this with confidence.

The ideal drop shot leaves no chance for return and is an outright winner. Even if your opponent reaches the drop shot, you may still win the point. Many times the player attempting to return a drop shot will hit into the net or out. Even if she does return the ball, the return may be a weak one that you can return for a winner.

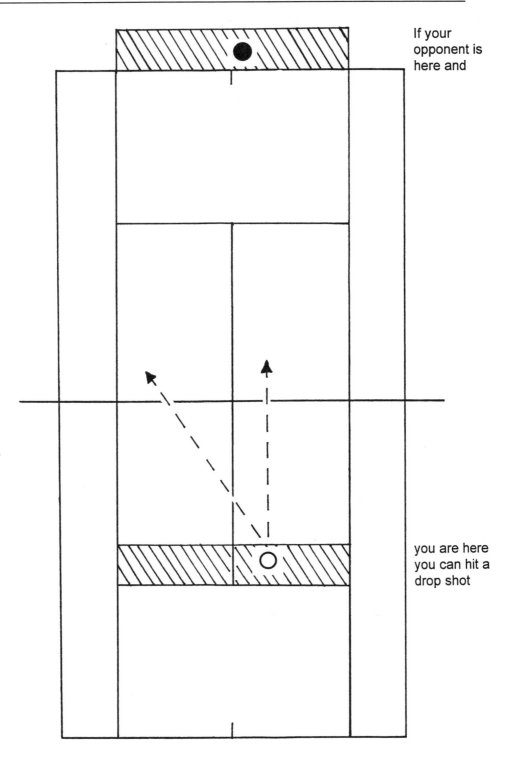

If your
opponent is
here and

you are here
you can hit a
drop shot

DROP SHOTS
YES

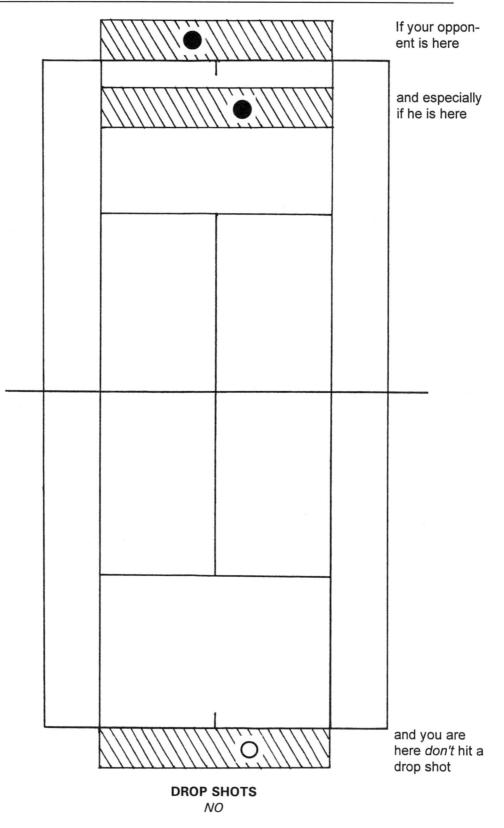

If your oppon-
ent is here

and especially
if he is here

and you are
here *don't* hit a
drop shot

DROP SHOTS
NO

The drop shot must clear the net and should bounce short and low. If it bounces high, your opponent will have time to reach it. Obviously, the most important thing is that it clears the net even if it bounces higher than you would like. Don't try to make your drop shot too perfect. This adds pressure to you that increases the probability of your hitting it in the net. It is better to have it clear the net—even if your execution isn't perfect—than to hit it into the net.

When to Use the Drop Shot Many players don't think of the drop shot as a high percentage shot. This is correct in most cases. However, when playing older players who have lost some of their court speed, the drop shot can be a more consistent winner. Not only do older players have difficulty reaching the ball, they become tired from all the running. When a player becomes tired, he makes more errors.

As a rule, hit a drop shot only when you are in the area of your service line. It is also advisable never to hit a drop shot on a big point or if you are behind in the game. The time to use a drop is when you have the lead in the game and want to take your opponent off guard.

When you have a lead in the game, you can try a drop shot —even if your position or situation isn't perfect. This will have the element of surprise. Even if you don't win the point, it can be upsetting to your opponent. One thing that makes the drop shot effective is its element of surprise. When you use it too often you are robbing it of its effectiveness because your opponent will begin to expect it. Remember that part of its effectiveness is the psychological effect it has on your opponent because of the element of surprise.

Other times that you might find the drop shot effective are against a weak serve, or as an effective way to bring a baseliner to the net. In addition, the drop shot is more effective on a clay court than on a hard court, since clay will not let it bounce as high.

If you are playing a fast, attacking opponent, the drop shot is almost useless, except in rare circumstances. Also, never hit a drop shot to an opponent who is already moving—he will get to the ball almost every time.

The drop shot is a low percentage shot in doubles. Rarely if ever use it, and then only against teams that tend to play from the baseline rather than keep one player at the net.

Placement If your opponent is deep in the crosscourt area, drop shot down the line. If he is in your down-the-line position, drop shot crosscourt. If he is in the center of the court, hit crosscourt, since he will have more difficulty reaching the ball as it bounces away from him.

Strategy   As soon as you hit a drop shot, *move forward*. Your opponent will have to hit up on the ball. If you are in the correct position, you may be able to volley to the open court for a winner.

Responding to a Drop Shot   It is important to learn how to respond to the drop shot. First, you must be alert so you can get to it. This is especially true if you are playing an opponent who uses a lot of drop shots. Then you have several options. You can hit a drop shot in return, but it must be a perfect drop shot since your opponent will probably be near the service line and thus better able to reach the ball. You can angle the ball sharply or hit deep down the sideline to the baseline.

Unless your opponent hits very hard ground strokes, you may find it a good tactic to rally from a position *slightly inside* the baseline. This will give you an extra jump in getting to the ball.

Have you ever started to run toward a drop shot and then decided that you couldn't get to it, so you stopped? Then after you stopped, you realized if you had continued forward you could have reached the ball? Of course you have. We all have. Remember, once you start toward the ball, *don't stop*. You may not get to it every time, but you will be surprised how often you can get to a drop shot when you thought you couldn't. An added bonus to this extra effort is, after you return a few, your opponent may decide not to use the drop shot against you.

Remember to concentrate on the strength of your return of a drop shot. The momentum of running forward, added to the normal pace of your stroke, will often make you hit the ball long.

LOB

Correctly executed, the lob is one of the most useful and versatile shots in tennis. It can bail you out of trouble and win points for you. It is particularly effective against slower players who may not be able to run it down. And even if they do, it will help tire them out more quickly than a more stationary volley.

Some players think only weak, inexperienced players use lobs. If you watch professional tennis players, you will see that lobs are used effectively by many strong, experienced players. It is not a "sissy" shot—it is a "smart" shot. The lob should be thought of as a variation of the ground stroke. Make sure that you hit the lob with a firm wrist so that it will go over your opponent's head.

When to Use a Lob When a player is rushing to the net, he is vulnerable to a crosscourt lob since he has to reverse direction and run back diagonally to reach the lob. Another advantage of the crosscourt lob is you are hitting into the longest part of the court. Even if your opponent can get to the ball, he will be in a difficult position from which to hit a good return.

The lob is most effective when hit from inside the baseline. If your opponent volleys short, the lob will not be expected. The volleyer will probably be closing in, and the lob will sail over his head as he is moving forward.

When you hit a good lob over your opponent's head and he has to scramble back for it, your best tactic is to come to the net. The odds are he won't be able to return the ball with any power, and you will have a chance to hit a winner. Your goal should be to hit perfect lobs, but if you don't—and even the pros can't do it every time—you may still win the point. At the club level players will often smash your lob in the net or out of bounds.

The lob is most often used against a net player, but it is also effective in response to wide angle shots. Wide angle shots will draw you out of position and make it difficult for you to get back in position if you hit an easy return to your opponent. Forget about trying to hit a great shot down the line—that is a low

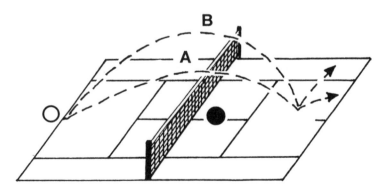

LOB
There are two kinds of lobs.
(1) Offensive lob (A) is hit just over the net man's reach. It is hit for a winner since the net man cannot get back soon enough to return it.
(2) Defensive lob (B) is hit high. Net man may be able to get back to return it, but it gets him away from the net. Also, use the defensive lob when you are out of position. It will buy you enough time to return to position.

percentage shot. Instead, lob deep and crosscourt. This will give you time to get back in position. *Lob when you're in trouble*; it will buy you time.

Doubles   In doubles, use the lob as a way to take the net away from your opponents. When one or both opponents retreat in an effort to retrieve the lob, that is the time for you and your partner to move forward and take control of the net.

Although lobs are not used often in doubles by pros, at the club level the lob can be a winning shot in doubles. In fact, for the average player, it should be regarded as a necessary weapon for winning doubles. This is especially true if the net man is hitting your service returns for winners. That's the time to lob over him—high and deep.

Responding to a Lob   If your opponent is a good lobber, you should be mentally prepared for a lob when you are at the net. Your best defense against a lob is to start moving back as soon as your opponent hits the lob—or preferably before he hits the lob, if he lowers his racket head in that telltale low back swing. Remember the tips on watching your opponent before he hits the ball in order to anticipate.

It's often best to let a high lob bounce before hitting it—especially if it's windy or the sun is in your eyes. When you do this, remember the ball will rebound at approximately the angle at which it hits the court. The means it will bounce *beyond* where it hits the surface of the court. Move back from that point and be ready to move forward so you will be in the correct position to hit the ball. It is always easier to run forward into the ball to establish position than it is to run backward to catch the ball as it moves away from you.

When an opponent hits a lob, the average player thinks he's in trouble. Instead, the reaction should be one of thanks. The lob provides you with the opportunity to hit an overhead winner. Go for it. Think positive.

OVERHEAD SMASH

Tennis players hit hundreds of thousands of forehands, backhands, volleys, and serves when they practice, but hit few overheads. Yet the overhead smash is one of the most important shots in tennis. To hit a sound overhead winner requires a lot of practice. And remember, to hit an overhead consistently you must watch the ball and get into the position to hit it.

The object of the overhead smash is to win the point immediately—with that shot. You win the point by smashing the ball with power or by placing it accurately out of easy reach of your opponent. The average club player may not be able to hit the ball with a lot of power and will win more points by using the latter strategy.

What to Do One problem many club players have with hitting overheads is that they let the ball get behind them. Moving back to hit a ball that is behind often forces them to hit the ball long. Avoid this by moving back quickly. Remember, it is better to move too far back and have to move forward to hit the ball, since it's easier to make adjustment of position by moving forward.

When getting ready to hit an overhead, try to position yourself where the falling ball would hit your chest if you didn't hit it. This will put you in the correct position to hit the ball. (One good technique that will help you judge a lob and hit more accurately is to point toward the ball with your free arm.)

When your opponent hits a high, deep lob you are not going to be able to smash it for a winner because you will be too far back in the court. Why risk making an error? Return it with moderate pace and good depth (close to the baseline) combined with accurate placement.

Don't hit an overhead too hard when it isn't necessary, and don't aim for over the lines. The average player will win more points with a medium-paced, accurately placed overhead than a cannonball that hits the fence. Play percentage tennis. Never hit any harder than necessary.

Many players, when they hit an overhead, relax and consider the point to be over. This is by no means a safe response. If you hit an overhead smash, your opponent will often be able to return the ball. You should be alert and get back in position. The point is not over until the ball is out of play. This cannot be stressed too many times; always assume that you will have to return the ball until the point is decided.

APPROACH SHOT

The time to hit an approach shot and come to the net is when your opponent hits a short ball that falls inside, or close to, the service line on your side of the court. The purpose of the approach shot is *not* to hit a winner, but to position yourself to hit a winner on the next shot.

It isn't necessary, or even desirable, to hit your approach

shot too hard. It's better to hit a medium-paced, well-placed approach shot than to hit a "bullet" because you are less likely to make an error. A slower approach shot also allows you more time to get to the net.

Usually the best way to hit an approach shot is to chip the ball. Once you've hit your approach shot you should *continue to move forward.* If you completely stop to make your hit, you'll never get to the net position in time.

The traditional approach shot is to your opponent's weaker side. Most often, but not always, this is his backhand.

If you find that your opponent's return shot consistently passes you as you approach the net, check to see if you are hitting your approach shot to the corners all the time. Try an approach shot down the center of the court right at your opponent. Jam him. This forces him to make a tough last minute adjustment and also takes away his angles.

Regardless of where you hit the approach shot, be sure you hit it with depth. This gives you more time to get to the net position and makes it less likely your opponent will be able to hit a passing shot.

Mental Pressure   It is possible to win at the net even if you are not a great volleyer. There is a psychological advantage to hitting an approach shot. This maneuver automatically puts your opponent in a defensive position.

An advantage of hitting an approach shot and moving toward the net is the adverse psychological effect it has on your opponent. In addition, the sight of you rushing to the net may cause your opponent to over-hit or make other errors if he takes his eyes off the ball to watch you coming to the net.

PERCENTAGE TENNIS

Percentage tennis is simply using the shot that has the best chance of success in the immediate point. Another way of saying this is that you want to use your immediate strength against your opponent's immediate weakness. In percentage tennis, try to hit your strongest shot as often as you can—if possible, hit it to your opponent's weak side.

One of the secrets of playing percentage tennis is getting into correct position to make your best shot. Don't loaf. Move quickly.

In any given situation there is usually one shot that is the percentage shot. Learn what these shots are and stick with them.

These are the "bread and butter" shots that work 90 percent of the time. Percentage tennis is more than just keeping the ball in play. Percentage tennis is simply using the shot that has the best chance of success in the immediate point. When you get a chance to put the ball away, that's a percentage shot.

Errors There are many reasons you make errors. The more of these reasons you can eliminate, the more you increase your chance of winning. Try to think of these things as things to avoid, then your percentage of wins will improve.

Sizzling first serves. Many first serves are errors because the player served too hard. The percentage player doesn't gamble by hitting low percentage sizzling first serves. He realizes that the purpose of the serve is to start the point—not end it with a fault.

Sensational returns of serve. Better players can often return a weak second serve for a winner. This is not, however, always a good percentage play for the average club player. The percentage return is a conservative crosscourt return. The object is to make a safe return.

Unnecessary risks. No matter how many sensational winners you hit during a match, they will amount to nothing if you make more errors as a result of attempting them. Play percentage tennis, and let your opponent go for the sensational shots—and the errors. Percentage tennis does not mean you should never take an unwarranted chance. Some risks are worth taking, but only in certain situations and only when you have the skill to make the shot that's required. Take a chance only when there is a good possibility of a payoff.

Hitting too close to the line. The percentage player recognizes that most points end because one player tried to hit the ball too low or too hard or too close to the sideline. Don't try to hit too close to the sideline. Don't aim for the sidelines. Aim for a point halfway between the singles sideline and the imaginary extension of the center service line. Give yourself a safety margin and always try to hit the ball deep. Play a steady, conservative game.

Looking up too soon. Because of the emphasis on watching the ball, there is the temptation to look up too soon after hitting the ball. This causes many players to look up *before* they hit the ball, ruining concentration on the shot and on the ball and causing errors.

Changing your mind after committing to a shot. Once you've decided what stroke you are going to use and where you are going to hit the ball, *do not change your mind*. When you change your mind after committing, you will almost always make an error.

Attempting shots you do not "own." When you are playing someone who is clearly better than you, don't try anything not in your repertoire. This will simply lessen your chance of winning. Don't beat yourself. Play your regular game of percentage tennis and you may pull off a big upset.

Wasting energy early on. Don't waste energy—mental or physical — on every point early in a match. If you do, you won't have enough left later when you really need it.

Losing concentration. It's a costly mistake to become so nervous on a big point that you try to do too much and over-hit. When you start to worry about possible negative results, your anxiety can have a detrimental effect on your tennis game. When you start making unforced errors, take a little pace off your shots until you regain your rhythm.

Becoming over-confident. The easier the shot, the more you need to concentrate to avoid making a mistake. In addition, if you make a good shot, the tendency is to relax. For example, many players who break their opponent's serve immediately lose their own serve. The usual reasons are either relaxing from over-confidence or suffering a letdown. At the same time, your opponent, who has just lost his serve, is concentrating extra hard to break back so he won't lose the set.

Giving up. When a player gets too far behind, he may just plain *give up*. Guard against this happening to you.

Keep the Ball in Play Consistency is the trademark of a percentage player and is the direct result of effective practice. To improve your consistency, ease off on your shots and don't go for winners too soon. Most errors occur when a player tries to hit a winner too soon, rather than waiting one or two shots longer for a higher percentage shot.

Many players, especially young players, equate how good they play with how hard they can hit the ball. If they hit it back twice they feel they have had a long rally. If you keep the ball in play three or four times, you'll beat the inexperienced hard hitter. "Bangers" hit for winners, but consistency will beat a banger every time.

If you keep the ball in play five or six times, you will beat almost everyone. Since most points are lost on errors, it is important to keep the ball in play until your opponent makes an error. Each time you hit the ball safely, you give your opponent another opportunity to make an error. Keep the ball in play to win.

Tactics There are some specific tactics to remember if you want to keep the ball in play. Playing percentage tennis and keeping the ball in play are the keys to playing winning tennis.

- When you are serving, get your first serve in. If you have to use your second serve, be sure it has good depth and placement.
- When you are receiving serve, be sure to get the ball in play.
- Once the ball is in play, keep it in play. Let your opponent be the one to make an error.
- The basic tactic winning games are based on is a steady baseline game using crosscourt shots.
- When you are winning, *speed up* your play. When you are losing, *slow down* your play.
- If you are losing badly, change your tactics. Vary your game. Vary the speed of the ball. If you are playing offensive tennis, switch to a defensive game. Change your placements. Above all, maintain a positive attitude.

Risks Playing percentage tennis does not mean that you never take risks. You need to take chances under certain circumstances. It makes the game more fun and keeps your opponent off balance The secret is not to take risks too often, to take them only when the odds for success favor you.

Take calculated risks. When you take a risk, there should be at least a fifty percent chance of your winning the point with that shot or close to a hundred percent chance of losing the point otherwise. If there is less than a fifty percent chance of your shot being a winner, don't try it. The odds are against you.

If you are serving and leading 40-love or even 30-love, you can afford to take an occasional risk. But if the score is deuce or love-30, revert to the basic strategy of keeping the ball in play.

Limit your risks to *one per point*. If you start taking several chances per point, you'll lose most of the time. Use a risky shot *only when it could be an outright winner* and you are already ahead.

When your risky shot *is* a winner, there is an additional bonus. It will discourage your opponent. He will be thinking about your *sensational* shot when he plays the next point, and the mental distraction may cause him to make an error.

PLACEMENT

Although all parts of a tennis game are important, intelligent placement of shots will win more matches for you than any other strategy. Accuracy is more important than power because accuracy wins points and matches. Your winning will depend more on the accuracy of your placements than any other part of the game.

The destination of a shot is more important than the speed. A weak shot to the *right place* is better than a hard hit ball to the wrong place. Victory comes from selecting where to hit the ball and then hitting it there.

There are many reasons good placement is so important to playing tennis.

- Good placement enables you to play your opponent's weakness.
- Good placement wins the point for you if your opponent can't reach the ball.
- Even if your opponent can reach the ball, he may be so rushed that he makes an error (known as a "forced error").
- Even if your opponent returns the ball, the return may be so weak that you close out the point.
- Even if your opponent makes a good return, he may be out of position for the next shot.
- Good placement causes your opponent to run more, taxing his endurance.
- Good placement allows you to vary your game. If the placement of all of your returns is too predictable it gives your opponent a big advantage. Vary your placements.

Where to Hit Decide where you are going to hit the ball and don't change your mind in the middle of a stroke. When you change your mind, odds are you'll make an error.

- There are many different kinds of strokes you can use, but there are only three places you can hit the ball. To the left, right, or down the middle. You can, of course, hit short or with more depth.
- Keep your opponent off balance by not playing a predictable pattern. *This does not mean you shouldn't play percentage tennis*. You can play percentage tennis and not be set in a pattern. You should have more than one response to any given situation.
- When you have to hit a shot while running toward either sideline, go crosscourt, unless you are going for a winner. The down-the-line shot opens up too much of your court.

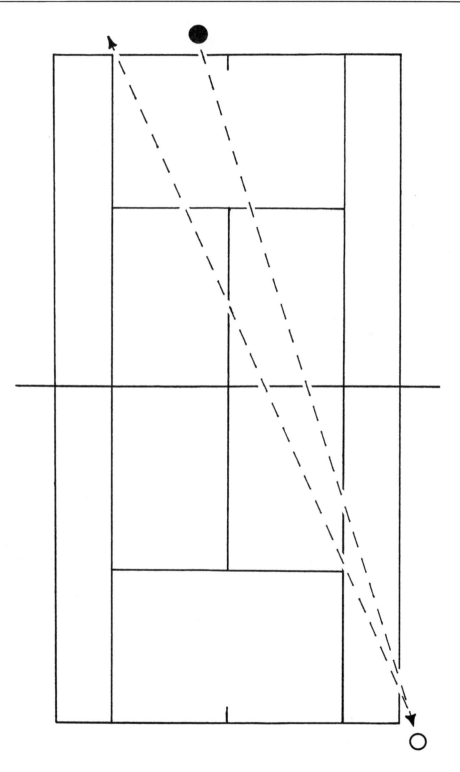

OUT OF POSITION RETURN

When you are out of position, return crosscourt. Return down the line only when hitting for a winner since it will leave too much of your court open.

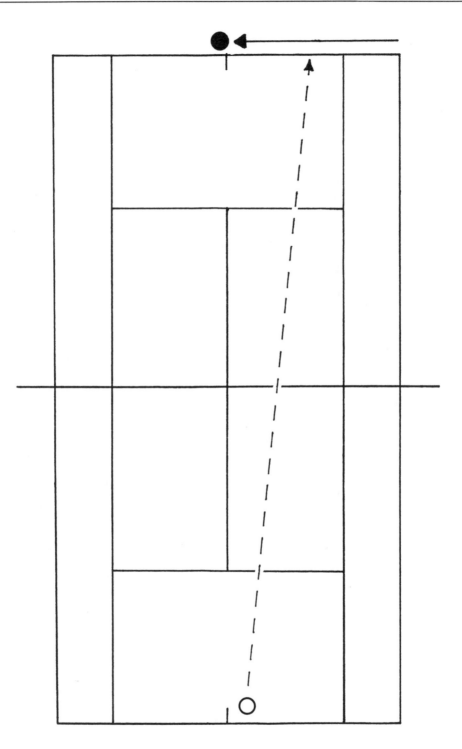

RETURN TO OUT OF POSITION OPPONENT

When you catch your opponent out of position and he is running to get back in position, hit behind him. This will "wrong foot" him and make it difficult for him to return the ball.

- When you and your opponent are trading shots from the baseline, the percentage shot is crosscourt. The diagonal is longer, there is more room to play the shot, the angle is tougher, and the ball crosses the net at the lowest point.
- Hit down the line only on approach shots, passing shots, or in situations where you want to exploit an opponent's weakness or to vary your style of play to keep him guessing.
- When your opponent is caught out of position and is running to get back in position, your best placement is to hit behind him. This will "wrong foot" him and make it difficult for him to get to the ball.
- When you hit a drop shot at a right angle to the net, all your opponent has to do is run forward to reach the ball. A more effective drop shot is one hit *diagonally* across the net, away from your opponent. When you do this your opponent not only has to run forward, but also to the side, so he has to run farther to reach the ball.
- One good response to a drop shot is another drop shot— when your opponent remains in the backcourt. If he is mid-court, a deep shot to either side could be a winner.
- Hit the ball deep and there will be little your opponent can do to hurt you. Don't aim too close to the line. Aim two or three feet *inside* the line. If, however, your shot falls inside the service area, you will be in trouble.
- In doubles, return serve crosscourt, except for an occasional down-the-line shot to keep the net man honest and an occasional lob over the net man's head.
- Even if you don't have a variety of different serves, use what you have and try to vary the placement. Placement of the serve is as important as the type of serve. If you hit your serve to the same place every time, the receiver will soon be able to return without any trouble. Try to keep him guessing.

Control

You will win almost every match where you maintain control and dominate your opponent. There may be some things you can't control. For example, the weather, or a good shot from your opponent. But you can—and must—control your reaction to these events beyond your control. Controlling your emotions is essential if you are to maintain your concentration.

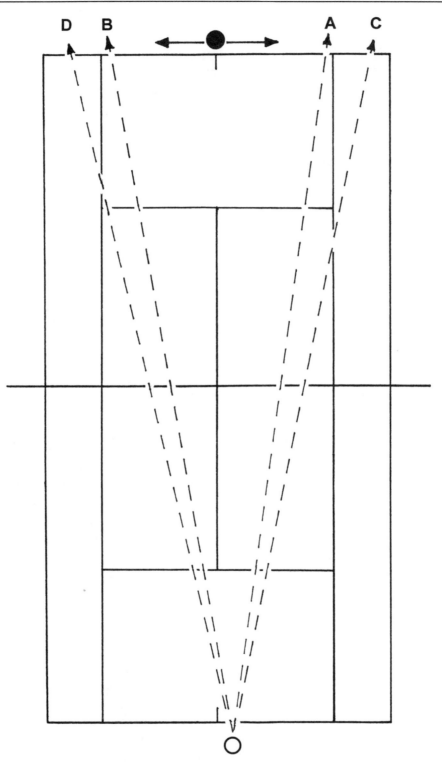

PLAY IT SAFE

Don't try to hit too close to the sideline. Aim 2 to 3 feet inside the baseline (A and B). C and D will lose the point for you.

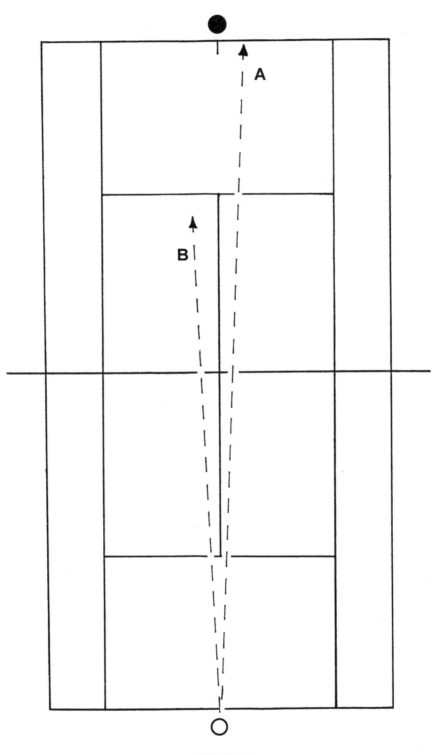

HIT DEEP

Hit deep to A and there is little your opponent can do to hurt you.
If you hit a short ball to B, your opponent may be able to hit a winner
or a good approach shot.

ERRORS

We have all made errors by mishitting the ball. In order to avoid repeating the mistake you should pause for a second and visualize how you *should* have hit the ball. At the same time go through the *correct physical motion* of the stroke you have just mishit. This practice (without actually hitting the ball) with both mental and physical aspects helps you to groove the stroke so you will be less likely to repeat the error. Unless you do this you may find yourself grooving the incorrect stroke.

THE NET

Every time you step on the tennis court, be prepared to play *two* opponents. Yes, that's right, two opponents. One of your opponents is the person on the other side of the net holding the racket. Your other opponent is the *net*, where most errors happen. When hitting a percentage shot, your first concern should be the net. The net is your enemy. Sometimes it almost seems the net reaches up and grabs your ball. Be sure your shots clear the net.

While I have always believed that more errors are made by hitting the ball into the net than by any other type of mistake, I did not have any statistical proof to support this belief. This led me to carefully chart the errors in fifty matches to document the prevalence of different kinds of errors. The results were even more dramatic than I anticipated.

- Forehand errors: Net 602, long 264, and wide 292.
- Backhand errors: Net 444, long 194, and wide 234.
- Players at the net: Net 84, long 22, and wide 16.

In all cases there were more net errors than long and wide errors combined. The net players made over two times as many errors hitting the ball into the net than hitting the ball long and wide combined.

This informal survey confirms the importance of concentrating on clearing the net. Think, "Clear the net." The cardinal sin on any point—no matter what your style of play—is hitting the ball into the net. That is the quickest way to defeat (and demoralize) yourself.

Have you ever had an opponent hit a return that you thought wasn't coming over the net but it did? Of course you have. We all have. *Assume* that every ball will come over the net until it actually hits the net. Always be in position to return the ball, should it come over.

13

Game Plan

A game plan is a strategy for utilizing your strengths and taking advantage of your opponent's weaknesses. A good game plan can be very helpful in maintaining your confidence and directing your energy. When all is said and done, the way to win tennis matches is to miss fewer shots than your opponent. A good strategy will help you do that.

It doesn't have to be complicated. It can be as simple as deciding to keep the ball in play until your opponent makes an error. A good game plan for the average player is to concentrate on hitting high and deep with a wide margin of safety to prevent errors. This will help keep the ball in play until your opponent makes an error. The plan can be more complex, but a simple plan is easier to execute and more likely to result in success.

Tennis isn't like bridge. Tennis is played best without conscious thought. This is why I have spent so much time talking about practice and about "grooving" your shots. This is also why it is important to have a game plan—and to stick with it. You have to react so quickly that there isn't time to debate all of the possible alternatives. You have to react in an automatic and almost unconscious manner based on your years of practice and experience — and your game plan. Knowing your opponent's strengths and weaknesses will help you prepare yourself, mentally and physically, for the match.

SCOUTING YOUR OPPONENT

You need to know something about your opponent's ability and style of play before you can design a good game plan. The more you know about your opponent and the way he plays tennis, the better chance you have of winning when you play against him.

It has been said that Max Schmeling saw that Joe Louis had a habit of dropping his left and was able to take advantage of this weakness. While a tennis player may not "drop his left," he usually has some recognizable weakness. Observe your opponent as he plays. When you see what his weakness is you will be able to hit him with a "knockout" stroke that will put him "down for the count," or at least for the point.

Scout your opponent when he is playing a match. Learn everything you can about your opponent *before* you play him. You don't want to use your first set trying to learn what your opponent can and can't do. As you observe him, notice the following:

- Notice his body language. Is he cocky and confident? Does he seem insecure?
- How is his serve? Is it strong or weak? What percent of his first serves does he get in? Does he just "tap" in his second serve? Does he always serve to the same location in one of the service courts?
- What about his ground strokes? Does he hit with topspin or does he chip or slice? Is his forehand or his backhand his strongest stroke? Does he run around his backhand?
- Is he a "banger" or a "pusher"?
- Does he rush the net or play a baseline game?
- Does he use a drop shot? Often? In what situations? How good is it? Where does he usually hit it? Does he move in immediately afterwards?
- When his opponent comes to the net does he try to pass him or does he lob? How good are his lobs?
- How good is his overhead? Where does he usually smash them?
- Is he patient? Does he keep the ball in play or does he try to end the point quickly?
- How does he react when he gets behind? Does he start hitting the ball harder and harder or does he take some pace off the ball and try to get back in the "groove"?
- Is he a good retriever? Does he try to get every ball? How fast is he in covering the court? How good is he at anticipating where his opponent's return will go? Does he have a "home base" to which he returns after every shot?
- Does he seem to follow a game plan? If he is losing does he seem to change his plan?
- How is his physical condition? His physical condition will determine, to some extent, his style of play and his weaknesses.

Doubles If you will be playing doubles it is also important to scout your
Opponents doubles opponents. Many of the things that apply to scouting
your singles opponent also apply to scouting your doubles opponents. Observe how they play as a team and try to learn the
answers to the following:

- Where and how does each one serve? Does one player have
  a weaker serve than the other?
- Which opponent has the weaker overhead? This will help
  you determine where to hit your lobs.
- Do they both lob?
- Do they both try to play the net or does one always stay at
  backcourt?
- Is one faster than the other?
- Does one poach? Does one never poach? How successful are
  they when they poach?
- Do they communicate with each other? Do they encourage
  each other? Do they seem to get along? Does one try to take
  the most shots or dominate play?

The more you see your opponents play, the more you will
know about their style of play, their weaknesses, and their
strengths.

Take advantage of every opportunity to scout other players.
Even if you are not scheduled to play them now, you may play
them at some future date. Even if you never play each other, you
may learn something to help develop your own game.

STRATEGY

Once you have scouted your opponent and detected his strong
and weak points, you are in a position to plan your strategy for
the upcoming match.

If your opponent is a much better player than you, there is a
chance of his winning no matter what you do. However, if you
and your opponent are nearly equal in ability, a good strategic
plan may make the difference between winning and losing.

Not all tennis players have the same degree of skill or type
of play, therefore a strategy that will defeat one player will not
necessarily defeat another. That's why it is important for you to
tailor your strategy to your particular opponent.

Here are some suggestions to help you plan a winning
strategy. Choose those that will work best for you.

- Keep your strategy simple and easy to follow.
- Play your own game, not your opponent's.
- You win by hitting medium-paced balls, with control.

- When you are behind, the worst thing you can do is try to hit harder and harder.
- Don't attempt shots that have only a marginal possibility of success.
- A key to turning defeat into victory is to make your opponent play a type of game he is not accustomed to.
- Play aggressively on your strong side and steadily on your weaker side.
- In most cases, it is unwise to start doing something differently just because your opponent is tired or injured.
- When you change your normal pattern of play, you often lose your rhythm and timing—and maybe the match.
- Keep your opponent deep enough and there will be few ways he can hurt you.
- Let your opponent be the one to change the direction of his shot during the rally. When the direction is changed, an error is more likely.
- Keep your opponent guessing and he will be half beaten.
- If your opponent's best stroke isn't too devastating, consider hitting two or three balls to his strength and then "bombing" to one of his weaknesses. Or reverse this procedure; hit several shots to his weakness and then bomb one to his strength.
- Go with your best shot even if it means going head on with your opponent's strength.
- When you can't out-steady your opponent, try to keep him off-balance. Come to the net unexpectedly, thus forcing him to make a good shot. Bring him to the net by hitting short, low balls and drop shots. Try spins and high lobs for a change of pace.
- If you are basically a defender or "pusher" you may be more successful if you occasionally attack.
- When you can't beat a "moon-baller" at his game consider rushing the net, or on a short moon ball move in and hit it with an overhead.
- There is a temptation to use too much "junk" on clay courts. The drop shot, the lob, and the use of spins are important, but so are the steady crosscourt shots.
- If you try too many tricks you may outsmart yourself.
- Guard against becoming frustrated when you are behind.
- Use the elements. While it's never a good idea to change drastically from what you do best, it is good strategy to use the elements as much as possible. This includes wind and sun. If your opponent is having problems with the sun and

you are a reasonably good lobber, then lob.

- Don't be predictable. While it is good to use primarily the strokes and placements with which you are most comfortable, do not set up a pattern of play that your opponent can anticipate. To keep your opponent from exploiting this type of play, vary your strokes and placements. Surprise him occasionally. A mixture of shots will keep your opponent off balance. This will keep him from getting his own strokes grooved.

Backup Game Plan In addition to having a game plan determined at the start of a match, it is reassuring to have a backup plan. Your game plan should not be chiseled in stone. If your plan is not working, analyze it. Try to determine why it's not working. Make the necessary adjustments to ensure success. If this doesn't work then use your backup plan. Make sure that you do not rush into changing your strategy. Sometimes changing strategy will not work to your advantage. This is something that only experience can teach you, but it is helpful to have an option to change your game plan—after you have given it sufficient time.

Changing Strategy It's never too late to change. If you have been playing the same type of game for ten years or more, you may believe it's too late to change. You're wrong. Maybe you shouldn't radically change your strokes, but you can certainly change your strategy. Think your way to victory by having a *winning strategy*.

SERVICE RETURN PLAN

In addition to an overall game plan, you should have a "service return" plan. You should decide ahead of time where and how you will return your opponent's serve. After the server hits the ball, you won't have time to decide which of several return options you will use. You can't consistently return the serve on a last minute impulse.

Your service return plan will, of course, depend on where and how the server hits the ball and how good a server he is. Decide ahead of time where you will hit the return if it is to your forehand and where you will hit it if it is to your backhand. Your plan may not work perfectly every time, but it will give you a big advantage over no plan at all. We talked about this in the chapter on serving.

PRE-GAME PREPARATION

The Boy Scout motto, "Be prepared," is also a good motto for the tennis player. Often the difference between winning and losing is preparation. The good player is always ready and will press the player who is unprepared. The player who is prepared for any eventuality is better able to cope with whatever happens.

The hour or so immediately before a match is especially important. Take this time to review your game plan and prepare your mind for the upcoming battle. You should have a game plan. The player who doesn't have a game plan plays every match the same way, and is often beaten by a player who has a plan.

Good preparation consists of information, skill, good physical condition, and a positive state of mind. It is essential for good performance. Remember that you begin every match with finite mental and physical reserves. Be prepared to conserve these resources for pivotal points in the match.

Equipment   Check your equipment *before* you start to play. Be sure you have all the equipment and supplies. Do this the night before the match. Make a list if necessary. Thorough preparation will eliminate this distraction so you do not have to contend with it on the day of the game.

Rackets and balls are not the only items to bring to the tennis court. Make certain you bring water, towels, a hat, sweatbands, bandages, and perhaps a chair.

Tournament preparation should begin long before you step on the court for your first match.

Warmup   The warmup is an important part of playing tennis. Tennis is a
and   sport of movement —usually rapid movement. There are quick
Cool Down   changes of direction, sudden stops and starts that place stress on the joints and the muscles of the body. These movements can result in injury, unless you warm up properly before starting to play.

There are several different schools of thought about the purpose of the warmup. There is general agreement that its primary purpose is to warm up and limber the body while you hit your strokes.

Rallying is not a substitute for warming up. It's important to start your physical warmup *before* you start to rally. Sudden exertion without a gradual warmup can lead to an abnormal heart rate and changes in blood pressure, which can be especially dangerous for older players.

You must put your joints through their complete range of motions to loosen up the tight connective tissue. This physical warmup gets the body physiologically ready for the greater activity of play. It also helps you avoid injury when play begins. A light sweat is a good indication that you have warmed up sufficiently.

Contrary to what many players think, stretching is not the way to start your warmup because your muscles are "cold." Research has shown that stretching is more effective if done after a brief period of exercise.

Before you start stretching, jog a little and do a little light calisthenics. Get the blood flowing—then do your stretching. Remember to pay special attention to your back and shoulder muscles.

When you do start to stretch, *don't overdo it*—never stretch to the point of pain. You are not trying to see how far you can stretch. Do the stretching slowly and easily. Do not bounce.

In addition to warming up before play, you must take the time to "cool down" after play. When your match is over, take time to stretch and walk around until your heart rate has returned to normal. This is especially important for older players.

Stroking It is important to use the warmup to practice your strokes, in-
Warmup cluding your serve. By doing this you'll know what's working for you that day and what isn't. Use the warmup to "groove" your strokes.

Some think that if you are playing a stranger you should not let him know how you play before the match starts. For example, if you are a drop shot artist, don't practice that shot during warmup. If you do, you risk losing the element of surprise when you use the drop in actual play.

Some players suggest you start warming up at the net. This puts you closer to your opponent and provides you with an unobstructed view of him. You will also seem in control when you are at the net and this may upset your opponent. In addition, you may delay his getting into his normal baseline rhythm.

It's best to start your stroking warmup slowly by using some *shadow* strokes. You can do this before you even step on the court. When you do start hitting the ball, begin with medium pace and gradually work yourself up to more stressful strokes.

If your opponent hits a hard shot toward the sideline during the warmup, don't run for it. After actual play begins is the time for hard running. Conserve your energy for that time.

Almost every player hits better during warmup than he

does once he begins play. Don't be intimidated if your opponent hits great shots during the warmup.

Use the warmup to study your opponent—how he hits his shots, etc. Hit different types of shots to different parts of your opponent's court. This will enable you to observe his reaction to different shots.

Cold Weather Warmup When you are playing in cold weather (and many avid players play in cold weather), your muscles remain tight and movement is restricted. It is even more important that you warmup properly before playing in cold weather. Try warming up *before* going outdoors. Also remember to cool down indoors.

There are other factors to consider when the weather is cold. Proper clothing and diet are the keys to cold weather comfort and safety. Layering keeps you warm by trapping heat. As you get warmer, you can take off the outer layers of clothing.

Eating more calories of complex-carbohydrate foods (such as pasta and whole grains) and calorie-dense foods (such as polyunsaturated fats) helps keep your body's core temperature regulated to keep you warm in the cold.

Determine Your Best Preparation There is no one right way to spend the hour or so before a match. Since players' personalities differ, what is right for one isn't necessarily best for another player. Try to determine what is best for you as you prepare for your match and do those things. The important thing is to get in the proper frame of mind. A set ritual prior to a tennis match prepares you for competition. Go off by yourself, get psyched up, and let the adrenalin start to flow.

Smile. You're going to be playing tennis; other people will be working.

IMPORTANT POINTS

The players who win consistently play all points as important points. Let me clarify what I mean. Although all points are important, there are certain times when it may be wise not to try too hard for a particular point. Do not let failure to exert yourself on one point become a rationalizing pattern of play, but be wise about conserving your energy. This is particularly important for older players who need to conserve their strength. For example, when your opponent is serving and leads 40-0, the odds are against you breaking his serve. *Don't give the point away*, but don't mentally or physically "go all the way" in the same manner you would on a more critical point. (If, however, it's set or match point, try your best to win it.)

While every point in a game is important, there are certain points that are absolutely critical. Become aware of them so you can turn the pressure on by exerting a little extra effort. Obviously, the most important point is the last point in a game since the winner of that point wins the game. The second most important point to win is the first point because it can give you a psychological advantage and may set the tone of the entire match.

Another important point is when the score is 40-30, or 30-40, because the next point will determine either who wins the game or will make the score deuce. In addition, pay close attention to your serve when you are serving and the score is 15-30. The next point can put you even if you win it. Lose it and you will be behind 15-40, giving your opponent two break points and a good chance to win the game.

Closing Out a Match Many players find it difficult to close out a match—even when they have a substantial lead. They are said to lack the "killer instinct." What happens is they lose their concentration.

You can't win unless you are able to close out the match. When you are ahead this should be easy, but it isn't for many players. They start thinking, "I've got a chance to win." Then they start waiting for their opponent to lose. But he doesn't. Instead, he wins.

When you are about to close out a match, *don't change your game*. Continue to play the game that put you in the lead. Keep calm and *concentrate*.

Your opponent will expect you to become more careful when you are trying to close out the match. Fool him, concentrate, and play the match out to the end the same way you've been playing.

Your opponent will have nothing to lose if you are close to winning, so he is likely to hit risky surprise shots. Don't let this upset you. If you do, you'll lose your concentration. Just keep playing your own game.

It's often easier to come from behind and win than to hold onto a lead.

Match Point When you have match point it's important to realize that your opponent is going to try harder than ever. He'll probably get to balls he ordinarily wouldn't reach. He'll probably make some sensational shots. That's why you have to raise the level of your own game on match point and maintain your concentration.

When you are leading 5-1 or 5-2 and have match point, it is *very important* not to fall into the trap of telling yourself that if you don't win that point or the game, it doesn't matter because you'll have several more chances to win. When you do, you lose your concentration and run the risk of seeing your lead evaporate to the point of losing the match.

It's hard to do, but when you're closing out a match, try not to think about the score, your opponent, or yourself. Don't think about the point you just lost or what will happen if your opponent wins the game. Just concentrate on the ball and play your usual game.

IMPORTANT GAMES

When you are serving and the game score is 4-5 or 5-6, the next game may determine who wins the set. If you lose that game, you lose the set. However, if you win that game, you will pull even. Conversely, if the score is 5-4 or 6-5 and you win that game you win the set. If you lose that game your opponent pulls even.

Every game is important, but in a close match the seventh game is more crucial than the others. It can mean the difference between 2-5 and 3-4.

On the next game after a long deuce game there is usually a letdown and in many cases the next game is a short one. Don't be the one to relax, even temporarily. Concentrate and you'll be the winner.

The first game after a long set is often seen as anticlimactic. This is especially true for the winner of the set. If you are the winner, try especially hard to win the first game in a new set. If you are the loser, this is your opportunity to catch your opponent napping.

Don't Drop Your Guard Do not get into the habit of relaxing when you are ahead and making it easy for your opponent to get points. This will build up his confidence and deflate yours. You can't afford to give your opponent the slightest edge. If you do, it may cost you the match. Remember, the best strategy is to play consistently and maintain your concentration. If you do this, you will be surprised how quickly your game improves.

14

Weather and Courts

There are certain conditions beyond your control that will influence your play. Learning how to play in different conditions will make you a better player. Weather and court surface are major factors for every player in every game.

WEATHER

Weather is an important factor in determining how well you play and how you ought to play. There are many variables: it may be hot or cold, dry or rainy, sunny or cloudy, calm or windy. Weather conditions and how you cope with them will often determine whether you win or lose.

Weather can be a plus or a minus depending on how you adjust to it and use it. Don't let adverse weather conditions frustrate you. You can't change the weather, but you can control your reaction to it. Use the sun, wind, temperature, and humidity to your advantage.

Sun The lob can be a most effective shot if it forces your opponent to look into the sun. Remember our discussion about spinning for serve and the options available? If you are a good lobber, you might consider choosing the side that allows you to use the sun to your advantage. Conversely, if your opponent is a good lobber, you might choose the "safe" side first.

If you are facing the sun when your opponent lobs, it is usually best to let the lob bounce. You can also use your free hand to screen the sun.

Wind There are three kinds of winds of concern in tennis. One blows from baseline to baseline, one blows from one side of the court to the other, and the other swirls around the court. Of course the intensity of the wind can vary from a gentle breeze to a steady gale to short gusts.

When hitting against the wind you should hit a little harder and deeper than normal. When hitting with the wind don't hit as hard as usual—let the wind help you out.

When serving with the wind there is a greater chance of hitting long. The velocity of the wind adds speed to the ball. In this situation take a little pace off your serve and aim lower.

When serving against the wind toss the ball more in front of you than usual—the wind will blow it back toward you. When serving into the wind there is a greater chance of hitting the ball into the net. The wind will put the "brakes" on the ball. Aim a little higher than usual to help compensate for this.

When the wind is gusting, forget about hitting hard first serves. Since the wind will move the ball around, it's a good idea to lower your service toss so the ball will not be as long in the air as usual.

When there is a cross wind, be especially careful not to aim too close to the sidelines. The wind may blow the ball out. This is particularly important to remember when you are hitting lobs. If the wind is swirling, it is best to try to hit down the middle of the court. Lob harder when lobbing against the wind. Use more spin when lobbing with the wind.

Keep the ball low on windy days because there is less turbulence close to the ground. In addition, spin can help you control the ball on windy days.

Remember to practice on windy days. If you only practice when conditions are "just right," you will not be able to play well in matches that occur under adverse weather conditions.

Heat   Heat affects your physiology. Dehydration and muscle cramps occur often during hot weather. This is of particular concern to the weekend player who is not in good physical condition.

Playing tennis in hot weather increases the player's perspiration rate. External factors such as humidity, air movement, amount and type of clothing, and intensity of heat all worsen the problem of dehydration. The prevention of dehydration is not only important to your performance, but critical to your health. Older players have to be especially careful when playing in hot weather.

You should "pre-load" your body's water supply by drinking a glass or two of water at least 15 to 30 minutes prior to play. Then replenish the lost liquid in your body by drinking some water at every change over. Cool water is best since it will leave the stomach sooner and exert the desired cooling effect.

Clothing Dressing properly when playing in hot weather is very important. Wear white, loose-fitting, breathable clothing. (Forget the denim and colored clothes some players are now wearing.) Also wear a hat or cap to protect your face and eyes from the sun's rays. All players should consider using a sunscreen.

COURT SURFACES

When playing tennis, you will not always have a choice of court surface. You should be knowledgeable about playing on all surfaces. The type of surface will often determine the type of game you play. Different players have individual preferences regarding court surface.

There are three basic types of traditional tennis court surfaces. These are: clay or manmade clay (like Har-Tru), hard (asphalt or concrete), and grass. (In addition, some indoor courts have a carpet-like surface.) Each of these surfaces has general characteristics that vary slightly from court to court within the same types of surface.

Clay Different types of clay surfaces play differently, and clay can be made to play slower by adding moisture to it.

On clay, the bounce of the ball is high and slow due to the loose, granular surface. This clay surface can slow down the hardest serve. You can also expect some bad bounces and skids when the ball hits the tape. The clay court favors the "retriever" or "pusher" and the player with a big bag of trick shots.

Patience, consistency, and stamina are the keys to winning on clay. Patience means waiting for the short ball you can attack, and consistency means keeping the ball in play.

The baseline player usually does better on a clay surface. If you hit with consistent depth, it will be difficult for your opponent to hurt you. This does not mean that a serve and volley player can't do well on clay. However, a lot of your offensive power will be negated by a slower surface. The big serve is not as important on clay as it is on other surfaces. You must be patient on clay and wait for an opportunity to hit a winner.

Hard Some hard courts play faster than others, depending on the surface finish. In all cases, however, the ball comes off the court much faster than on clay. Fortunately for the receiver, a predictable bounce offsets the speed factor.

This surface is best for the aggressive serve and volley player. This does not mean the baseline player can't do well on a hard court, but he must be able to hit passing shots and lobs —and be willing to come to the net when he has the opportunity.

Grass   Grass courts vary since different types of grass are used in different areas and the weather affects the condition of the court. On grass, the ball bounces low and fast with an occasional bad bounce, because the turf wears down with constant play, creating bald spots.

This is another surface that favors the aggressive serve and volley player. Few baseliners do well on grass.

Indoor   Indoor courts are the most varied in terms of surface. Some indoor courts have hard surfaces and a few are even clay, but most indoor courts have a "carpet" type surface. There are many types of carpet material used for indoor courts, and the playing characteristics depend on the type of material and the weave. Other indoor surfaces are rubber. The artificial lighting used indoors can also affect your play.

GAME STRATEGY

The type of surface you play on and the weather both help determine your game strategy. Play the type of game that best suits the court surface you are playing on when you "own" that game. Otherwise, play the game with which you are most comfortable and do the best you can.

Prevailing weather conditions may determine if you will be able to play your normal game or if you will have to change your game plan. When making your game plan, notice all the weather conditions. The weather will also affect your opponent and how he will play.

15

Doubles

Good teamwork is the secret of winning doubles. You and your partner have to think and play as a team. Many players think they are playing doubles when they are really two players playing singles on a doubles court.

Not all players are equally good at playing doubles. To be a good doubles player you have to *want* the ball to come to you so you can hit it. If you hope the ball *won't* come to you, then you will not be a good doubles player.

COMMUNICATION

One of the primary causes of failed marriages is lack of communication. The same is true of failure in the game of doubles. This is why it's so important to keep the lines of communication open. It's easy when you are winning, but it's an effort when you are losing. The way to change the game is to be supportive, keep talking, and try to figure out a game plan that will change the results.

Never moan, look unhappy, or criticize your partner when he makes an error—he didn't do it intentionally. This does not mean you shouldn't offer constructive suggestions to your partner. Hopefully, he will also be able to offer helpful advice to you.

Not only is it important to communicate, you must be sure that the communication is positive. Never criticize your partner when he makes an error. Just remember that everyone—even you — makes an occasional error. No one — especially your partner—makes an error on purpose.

Don't watch your partner hit the ball. Watch your opponents, and you'll know where the ball is going and which one of them is preparing to make the return shot.

When playing singles you may have an off day. We all do.

Note that both players are active with their eyes on the ball.

When playing doubles the odds are greater that at least one of you will have an "off" day — after all, there are two of you. Don't let this get you down. Keep playing to the best of your ability and the tide may turn. Your opponents may start making errors.

Let your communication be a message of encouragement. Your teamwork will improve, and you and your partner may become winners. In doubles, it is an inescapable fact that you win or lose as a team.

DECISIONS

Choice of whether to play in the deuce or ad court is the first decision doubles players have to make, and one of the most important. Each player's strengths and weaknesses should be considered when making the choice. It is very important that each player be satisfied with his side of the court. If both players always want to play in the deuce court—or the ad court—maybe they shouldn't be doubles partners.

The better player should be the aggressive one. If your doubles partner is the weaker player, you should try for more winners. In doubles, simply keeping the ball in play will not always work. If you simply keep the ball in play, your opponents will play the next shot to your partner. If he is a significantly weaker player, he may make an error and lose the point.

Which player on a doubles team should return a down-the-center shot is a question that frequently presents a problem. If the shot is *clearly* closer to one player than the other, then obviously, the closer player should hit it. Otherwise, the general rule is that the player who hit the previous shot should return the center shot.

Game Plan In doubles, as in singles, it is important to have a game plan. In doubles, however, there are two players on the team and it's important that they *both* know and agree on a game plan. If the game plan is changed, each player must understand that there has been a change and what the change is, and be committed to following through on the change.

FIRST SERVES

There are certain fundamentals that should be followed in all doubles play. Foremost is to get the first serve in. In doubles it is psychologically, as well as tactically, important for the server to get his first serve in every time. Even if the first serve is no harder than the second serve, the receiver will often subconsciously assume it will be harder to return than a second serve. A consistently good first serve will probably win the average doubles team more points than any one other thing.

NET PLAY

Championship doubles are not played from the backcourt. While some points — even some matches — may be won from the backcourt, almost all are decided at the net. Try to get to the net before your opponents.

When you are at the net, you should concentrate on protecting the center, not the sidelines. Most of the action will be down the center. Also, it is important that you create the impression that you know what you are doing by always looking confident and composed. If you do this your opponents may hesitate to hit the ball to you — and perhaps they will make an error.

Backhand return with both players close to the net.

SPECIFIC TIPS

- The average club player will not be able to hit a forceful down-the-line shot with any degree of regularity. Even if you have edged toward the center, when your opponent hits his down-the-line shot, you will often be able to block it back.
- If one of the opposing players is so weak as to be ineffective, hit most shots at him. If one is only slightly weaker than the other, it is probably better to play a traditional doubles game.
- When playing doubles, don't forget to hit an occasional shot down-the-alley. This will not only keep the net man "honest," it may win some points. Even more important, it will help keep the middle open for your down-the-middle shots.
- If one opponent is at the net and the other back, always hit to the one in the backcourt. Even when both are at the net, hit to the one who is farther back.
- Always hit down the middle if there is any doubt in your mind where to place your return.
- Hit most overheads down the center, but right-handers can hit the ball to the right and left-handers to the left.

Strong left-handed return.

POACHING

The first object of poaching is to hit a winner off any slow, high floater. The second object is to intimidate the receiver by threat of a poach, causing him to make an error.

Timing is crucial to the successful poach. When you poach, move *forward* as well as sideways. Poaching is like "cutting the ball off at the pass." You can't poach successfully if you are late moving to the ball, or if you fail to hit the ball for a winner.

When you poach you must anticipate and be alert and ready to move when the receiver hits the ball. You must not, however, move too soon. If you do, you will either overrun the ball or the receiver will see you move and will be able to hit behind you.

Some doubles teams find it an advantage to have prearranged signals when the net man is going "all out" to poach or feint, etc. Usually the signal is given by different "hand signals" behind the back of the net man. It is essential, of course, that the server understand and acknowledge the signals.

Receiving Poaches When you are playing against an aggressive poacher, you must "keep him honest" by hitting an occasional shot down the line on your return of the serve. Do this early in the match and continue to do it with some regularity. This may shake his confidence.

If the server's partner keeps poaching successfully on your return of the serve, then vary your return. You can defeat this behavior by lobbing over his head.

Feinting   A part of good poaching is the *feint*. Make the receiver think you are going to poach, then don't. Make him think you aren't going to move, then poach. This keeps the receiver confused. Don't let the receiver forget you. Make your presence known by constantly feinting.

Poaching in doubles can win points — if you are a good poacher. But fake poaching, or feinting, is a good tactical weapon even if you aren't a good poacher.

One purpose of the feint is to cause the receiver to take his eyes off the ball. Just a momentary distraction can cause him to make an error.

If you make a fake poach by moving a couple of feet toward the center, you will be surprised how often the receiver will hit the ball wide as he tries to keep it away from what he perceives to be a legitimate poach.

Plan Your Poach Ahead of Time   You will not be able to poach successfully if you always wait until the last moment to make the decision. Make up your mind ahead of time whether you are going to poach or not—depending, of course, where the serve lands.

16

Winning Tennis

The best advice I ever had on how to play winning tennis came, not from a teaching pro, but from my wife, who doesn't even play tennis.

One day she said, "I'll tell you how you can win every time you play tennis."

"Good," I said. "I'd like to know."

KEEP THE BALL IN PLAY

"All you have to do," she said, "is hit the ball back one more time than your opponent does."

Of course, she's right. If I did that, I would win every time. What she was actually saying, although she didn't express it in these words, was *keep the ball in play*.

You win by keeping the ball in play because every time you hit the ball back, you give your opponent another opportunity to make an error. And a point that's won because your opponent made an error counts the same as a point you make by hitting a winner.

REDUCE ERRORS

Contrary to what spectators (and most players) think, nobody wins a tennis match; somebody loses the match because of the errors he makes.

We all tend to remember the aces, the overhead smashes, and the sensational passing shots down the line. What we don't remember are all the *errors that actually determine the winner*.

You may doubt that this is true, especially when the players are top-ranked pros. I had my doubts too, until I charted actual matches. I have now charted dozens of matches at both amateur and professional tournaments as well as college and high school matches.

Error Statistics Perhaps some statistics from actual matches will illustrate why nobody wins and somebody loses. The following figures are based on matches that I observed where the players were fairly evenly matched.

On the average, 73.7% of the points lost in a match were lost because of errors. Only 26.3% of the points were actually won. These percentage figures clearly show that it's not winning placements and aces that determine the winner. It is errors. The player who makes the most errors will lose.

This doesn't mean the winner doesn't make errors also. It just means that the winner makes *fewer* errors than the loser. In fact, even the winner makes more errors than he makes winning shots. The average number of points lost by the winner in a match because of errors was 32.8. However, the average number of points in a match lost by the loser was 40.9.

At the 1991 Lipton International Championship Tournament, David Wheaton defeated Stefan Edberg 6-3, 6-4. In this match Edberg hit 17 winners, but made 38 errors. We'll score this -21 (17 winners less 38 errors). Wheaton hit 23 winners and 29 errors for a score of -6.

In the finals of the same tournament, Jim Courier defeated Wheaton 4-6, 6-3, 6-4. In this match Wheaton hit 35 winners, but made 64 errors for a -29. Courier hit only 24 winners, but made only 39 errors for a -15. In this match Wheaton actually hit 11 more winners than Courier, but he lost because he made 25 more errors. Note that both players made more errors than winners.

The same holds true for women players. For example, in the finals of the 1991 Virginia Slims of Florida Tournament at Boca Raton, Gabriela Sabatini defeated Steffi Graf 6-4, 7-6. In this match Graf hit 23 winners, but made 57 errors for a -34. Sabatini hit 27 winners and made 55 errors for a -28. (Again, both players made more errors than winners.)

The closest match I charted was a 1991 Chicago Indoor Tournament match between John McEnroe and Malivai Washington. The score in this match was 7-6, 6-7, 6-4, and the error score was McEnroe -20 and Washington -21. Had Washington made only two or three fewer errors, he might have won.

I recently observed a men's college match where the score was 6-3, 7-6 and the winner had a -29 and the loser a -31. This was another close match where the loser might have won if he had just made three or four fewer errors.

In a recent women's college match, both the winner and the loser hit 15 winners, but the loser made 59 errors, compared to only 36 errors for the winner. Thus the score was -44 to -21.

In a recent boy's high school match the loser actually hit 27 winners while the winner only hit 13 winners. The difference was the loser hit 74 errors while the winner made only 59 errors, so the minus score was 46 to 47. Very close, but the errors determined the winner.

The above ratios are typical of the dozens of matches I have charted. I have yet to chart a match where winners exceeded errors. This was true whether the players were men or women, professionals or amateurs, college or high school players.

As I said above, nobody wins; somebody loses. So, if you want to win, you do it not by hitting more winners than your opponent but by making *fewer errors*. Winning doesn't just happen. It's *what you do* that makes winning happen.

After all is said and done, you win by hitting the ball back one more time than your opponent. You do this by keeping the ball in play. As my wife said, "Hit the ball back one more time than your opponent does." Do this and your opponent will eventually make an error. Remember, nobody wins, somebody loses. Let it be your opponent.

As long as the ball is still in play the point is not over. Even if you are not able to hit a forcing shot, get the ball back. The secret of winning tennis matches, especially at the club level, is to let your opponent make the errors. This is another way of saying, "Keep the ball in play."

The ingredients of winning a game are consistency, control, accuracy, placement, and appropriate aggressiveness.

Most club players lose because they hit the ball too hard and too close to the line. Let your opponent be the one to try the high-risk shots and you'll be the winner.

BELIEVE YOU CAN WIN

You can't just hope you'll win. It doesn't work that way. If it did we would all be winners. You have to decide upon and take specific action to win. Have a plan, based on what you can execute and the strengths and weaknesses of your opponent. If you want to win, you must *believe* you can win. Winning and losing are both habits. The more you win, the more you *expect* to win —and the more you *will* win.

HOW YOU WIN

You win tennis matches by doing two things. First, do what you *want* to do and *can* do. Second, make your opponent do the things he *doesn't* want to do or *can't* do.

Although good physical condition is a necessary ingredient of winning tennis, there are other factors that are just as essential. These include hand-eye coordination, anticipation, and mental toughness.

You will win by playing percentage tennis. This is especially true on important points. You will never be a winner if you play by rote or habit and don't use your head.

The secret of winning big points is to keep the pressure on, but not to risk an error unnecessarily.

The way to win against players who are your equal in ability —or even better—is to hit a medium-paced ball with control. If you want to win, you can't sacrifice your control for speed.

Winning not only depends on how well you play, but on how well your opponent plays. Of course, how well you play will often affect how well your opponent plays.

If you really want to win, you can't worry about how you look as you play, or what others will think of you, or what the spectators might think. To play winning tennis you have to enjoy playing. Winning is more fun than losing.

Winners go for every ball, no matter where it is. That's the reason they are winners. If you do this you will be surprised at the number of balls you will get to.

You will have a much better chance of winning by outmaneuvering your opponent than by trying to outpower him.

Winning tennis matches depends not only on how well you execute your strokes, but how well you plan the placement of your shots in relation to your opponent's strengths and weaknesses.

There is only one way to guarantee you will be a winner every time you play tennis. Always play to the best of your ability and be a good sport about it. When you do this, you'll be a champion—even if you don't win the tournament.

THINK LIKE A WINNER

If you want to win, you have to *think like a winner*. You must stop making up alibis and excuses for losing. You've got to think positively and visualize winning. Winners see what they *want* to happen. Losers see what they *fear* will happen.

Winning tennis matches is more than just a matter of hitting good shots. It consists of winning all the points you can. *Never* concede a point or a game. Hang in there.

Winning is a habit just as losing is. The more you win, the more you expect to win and the more you will win. Success breeds success and when you're winning you will probably continue to win. Conversely, when you're losing you will probably continue to lose unless you have enough mental toughness to keep losing from affecting you.

All points are crucial and each one you win brings you closer to winning the game. Someone is going to win each point. Believe it will be you and go for it.

Winning at tennis is not determined by whether you are a "good guy" or a "bad guy." That only determines your popularity on the court. A nice guy can win if he is the better player and lose if he isn't. The same goes for the bad guy.

If you win the first set, the odds favor your winning the match. Knowing this should strengthen your confidence.

ALWAYS PLAY YOUR BEST

There are many players who want to win, but not enough to pay the price. You have to really want to win to be a winner and have the tenacity to persist in the face of adversity. Don't be satisfied to beat your opponent 6-2 or 6-3 when you could beat him 6-0 or 6-1. Play to the best of your ability every time you play. When you play less than your best, it may become a habit—and when you need your best it may no longer be there.

If hitting winners is more important to you than winning the match, you won't be a winner. You will win points if you ease off a little and try not to go for winners too soon.

There's a time and a place for every shot. There's a time to keep the ball in play and a time to put the ball away. The winner knows the difference.

STRIVE TO IMPROVE

You become a winner by *improving*. If you never improve, the players who are beating you now will continue to defeat you. The key to improvement is to admit that you need it. There is always room for improvement. If you think you "own a shot" but don't, you will never improve that shot. Be realistic. Evaluate your game. Practice those things that need improvement. Don't be too proud to ask for—and accept—advice.

You improve your game with determination, persistence, and patience. The greatest of these is patience. Don't become discouraged or let temporary setbacks deter you from your goal. Be patient and you'll become a winner.

If you are nervous about a big point, you can be sure your opponent is too. Tennis is a mental game. Stay mentally tough. Tennis is also a game of percentages. Select the high-percentage shots. Do these two things and you'll win.

If you think you can't, you won't try. Don't think about what you can't do. Think about what you *can do*.

STRATEGY

The famous military strategist Karl von Clausewitz said the key to winning wars is to isolate the "center of gravity." The center of gravity is that point to which you should apply your decisive efforts to achieve maximum results. This same principle can be applied to winning tennis "wars." In a tennis game, the center of gravity is that point where your opponent, the "enemy," is weakest. Discover your opponent's weakness and keep pounding it until he "surrenders." Whenever possible, scout your opponent and use that information to help you plan your most effective strategy.

HELPFUL HINTS AND CAUTIONS

There are many ways to play tennis and more than one correct way to hit the ball. The wise player seeks to find the way that best suits his physical and mental make-up. Some general suggestions include:

- Try for an early lead. Get ready quickly. Concentrate on getting in position to hit the ball.
- When you are in a baseline rally, be sure the ball clears the net. If it doesn't, you've lost the point before it really begins. The net is your enemy.
- It's better to hit the ball high over the net rather than low, and long rather than short. You'll make fewer errors if you do this and will be more likely to keep your opponent on the defensive.
- Keep the ball in play to give your opponent a chance to make an error—and he will. No one can hit winners all the time.
- Simplify and limit your options. Don't take a chance just to be flashy or to try to impress spectators with how hard

you hit the ball. Forget going for spectator winners and stick with percentage shots.

- The way to win any match is to play within your recognized limits using the shots you can make.
- There are two ways to play winning tennis. Use your strong shots as much as possible and play to your opponent's weakness.
- If you are behind, scramble for everything and keep the ball in play. Keep calm and decide if you need to change your game.
- Instead of running after a ball parallel to the baseline, run to the ball on an *angle* to the baseline. This will get you to the ball earlier, and it creates a greater angle for your return.
- If your opponent has a good, solid baseline game, break up his rhythm. Hit soft shots or lobs. Run him from side to side or up and back. Give him the unexpected and keep him off balance.
- When you are pulled wide, don't try hard for winners. Play percentage tennis. If your opponent comes to the net, hit a lob. If he stays back, also hit a lob or a deep topspin shot. Don't try for anything but depth.
- If you continue to make smooth percentage returns, you'll eventually get the opportunity to win the point.
- One way to protect your weak side is to hit the ball high and deep.
- When a ball is obviously out, don't hit it, but if there is any doubt that it may be out—and you can hit it—then hit it. There is no worse feeling than when a ball you could have hit—but didn't—drops in.
- No matter what the level of your game, you must play one point at a time.
- The best way to play against a "pusher" is with patience. Don't let him change your game. Keep hitting deep and wait for the inevitable shot that you can put away. Bring him to the net with a drop shot. Hit short, angled shots so he will have to run up and back as well as side to side. Push back to "pushers."
- When you hit a good lob, don't forget to move to the net.
- If your opponent hits a high lob, it may be best to let it bounce before returning it, especially if the sun is in your eyes or if it is windy.
- Move back if your opponent is hitting deep with heavy topspin.

- Take deep, slow breaths between points.
- Changeover time should be used for something besides drinking water. It's time to rest and relax and also to analyze the match, especially if you are losing.

  If you have a regular opponent who is close in ability there will be temporary ebbs and flows in your games with each other. Even if you defeat this opponent on a regular basis, if there isn't a great deal of difference in your playing ability, there may come a day when he will defeat you. Even the number one seed can be defeated—and often is. As the cowboy said, "There's never been a horse that couldn't be rode or a man who couldn't be throwed."
- For every action on your part there will be a counteraction by your opponent.
- There are many reactive players, but none are champions.
- Even the best players have highs and lows during a match.
- There are many good players who don't win.
- Players who win the first set generally win the match.
- The point is not over until the ball is out of play.
- All players like to play at their own pace and are uncomfortable having to play at any other pace.
- The player who relaxes or becomes careless when he is ahead is likely to lose the match.
- The player who tries to hit shots he "doesn't own" will make many errors.
- Know what you can and can't do on the court. Don't beat yourself by trying something you can't execute.
- Don't pick up and reinforce bad habits. If your muscles have programmed a bad habit, it is extremely difficult to reprogram and break that bad habit.
- Don't give your opponent a shot he likes to play. Don't let him play the game he prefers if you can possibly force him to play any other.
- Don't get caught admiring a great shot you just made—it might come back. Always be prepared if it does. Assume that every shot will be returned.
- Don't gamble by being more aggressive than necessary. Play percentage tennis.
- Once you've decided where you're going to hit the ball, don't change your mind. Concentrate on the ball and carry through on your decision.
- Don't over-hit, regardless of the stroke you are using. When playing someone obviously better than you, you will probably be tempted to hit harder than you usually do.

This is a common error on the part of the average player. Resist this temptation and stick with the shots you are capable of making.

- Don't forget that patience is required to win a point.
- Don't try to blast your opponent off the court when he is out-steadying you. You will make too many errors when you try to do this. Just keep the ball in play and hope for him to make an error.
- Don't suddenly start doing something different just because your opponent gets injured or is tired. Don't change your game when you are in a position to close out the match. Obviously, what you have done so far in the match is working, so don't change it.
- Don't try a drop shot on set or match point because it is the one time when your opponent will go all out to get the ball.
- Don't try to play a serve and volley game until you are able to control the depth and direction of your ground strokes.
- Don't wait to see if your return is in or out. Assume it's in and get moving so you'll be in position to return the ball if you have to.
- Don't try to hit winners from behind the baseline.
- Don't let your opponent see if you are tired. This will encourage him.
- Don't try to out-lob a lobber, out-hit a slugger, or out-dink the touch artist.
- Don't let it get you down when you lose. Realize that you can't win 'em all. No one can.
- Don't compose winning headlines until after you win.

SELF-EVALUATION

There are many reasons why you may lose. Ask yourself if you are doing any of the following:

1. Are you willing to pay the price for success?
2. Do you lose your concentration?
3. Do you lack confidence?
4. Do you fail to keep your eye on the ball?
5. Do you take unnecessary chances?
6. Do you try shots you "don't own"?
7. Do you let your opponent psych you?
8. Do you lose your patience?
9. Do you keep the ball in play?
10. Do you practice?

11. Do you have a winning strategy?
12. Do you get back in position soon enough?
13. Do you choke?
14. Are you in good physical condition?
15. Do you hit the ball too hard, or too high, or too low?
16. Do you make mental mistakes?
17. Do you sacrifice accuracy for power?
18. Do you have a routine?
19. Do you let bad calls upset you?
20. Do you give up?

TEN COMMANDMENTS OF WINNING TENNIS

1. Keep your eye on the ball.
2. Keep the ball in play.
3. Play percentage tennis.
4. Concentrate on the game.
5. Get your first serve in.
6. Stay mentally tough.
7. Scout your opponent.
8. Have a game plan.
9. Stay in good physical condition.
10. Never give up.

CONCLUSION

Remember, playing tennis is supposed to be fun. This awareness will help put the sport in proper perspective.

And laugh. Laughter is like internal jogging that relaxes muscle tension and releases beta-endorphins, the feel-good hormones.

And smile. Research shows that smiling can affect your mood. If you smile, it is almost impossible to get mad. And smiling increases blood flow to the brain.

Perhaps a smile and a little laughter will enable you to enjoy the game a little more the next time you play.

So smile. And laugh. It's only a game. Enjoy it. And good luck. Remember, you are never too old to play tennis, and never too old to start.

Glossary

ACE—A winning shot that is not touched by the loser's racket.

AD COURT—The "backhand court" for a right-handed player.

ALLEY—The 4 1/2 foot area on each side of the singles court that makes the court playable for doubles.

APPROACH SHOT—The shot that is hit when a player is advancing to the net position.

BACKCOURT—The area of the court between the sidelines and from the service line to the baseline.

BACKHAND—For a right-handed player, all strokes hit from the left-hand side of the body. For a left-handed player, all strokes hit from the right-hand side of the body.

"BANGER"—A player who tries to "kill" every ball.

BASELINE—Line at each end of the court parallel to the net.

CENTER LINE—The line separating the two service boxes, often reappearing as a stub on the baseline.

CHANGEOVER—The act of changing sides at the end of every odd game.

CHIP—A low sliced ball of medium speed that is not a drive or a dink.

COURT SURFACE—The material covering the top of the playing area (court). May be clay, hard, grass, or other.

CROSSCOURT—Hitting the ball diagonally from one side of the court to the other at an angle across the net.

DEUCE—An even score of 40 apiece.

DEUCE COURT—The forehand court of a right-handed player.

DINK—A stroke that drops the ball softly into the opponent's court (usually close to the net).

DOUBLE-FAULT—When both serve attempts are errors, the point is awarded to the receiver.

DOUBLES—A match with two players on each team.

DROP SHOT—Usually a softly hit, carefully aimed shot that

falls just over the net where the opponent has a hard time reaching it.

ERROR—A shot that does not go into the proper court or does not clear the net.

FEINT—A slight movement made by a player to make the opposing player think he is going to change position when no position change is made.

FLOATER—A slow moving high ball.

FOLLOW-THROUGH—The path of the racket after it has hit the ball.

FOOTWORK—The way a player moves his feet to get into position to play a shot.

FOREHAND—A forward stroke played by a right-handed player on his right side or by a left-handed player on his left side.

FRONT COURT—The area of the court between the net and the service line.

GAME—Play between two opponents (or teams of two) that is scored and is either won or lost by one opponent (or team).

GAMESMANSHIP—The use of legal tactics to upset your opponent.

GROUND STROKES—A stroke in which the ball is hit after it has bounced once.

HALF-VOLLEY—A ground stroke played immediately after the ball has bounced.

LET—A serve that hits the net cord but falls into the correct service court. Any point that is disputed or interrupted and called a let by the official. Let points are played over and are not credited to either player or team of players.

LOB—A stroke where the ball is hit high into the air in order to land as close to the opposing baseline as possible.

MATCH—A competition between two players or teams of players. In conventional scoring, a match is won by the player or team of players winning two out of three sets.

MIDCOURT—The middle section of the court in the vicinity of the service lines.

MOON-BALL—A stroke, similar to the lob, where the ball is hit from one baseline high into the air to the opposing baseline.

NET—The material stretched across the middle of the court that divides it in half. The net is usually made of a rope-like netting, but sometimes is a metal or wire-like material. The top of the net is 3 feet high in the middle of the court and 3 1/3 feet high at each sideline.

"NO MAN'S LAND"—The area between the service line and the baseline. This is a position particularly vulnerable to a variety of shots and is not a good position in which to remain.

NET GAME—A game played primarily at the net.

OPEN FACE—A racket that is angled up, toward the sky.

OUT—The call when the ball is outside of the boundary lines of the court.

"OWNING" A SHOT—The ability to hit (and place) a shot accurately and consistently.

OVERHEAD—A shot that is over the head of a player and that must be returned with a service-like motion.

PACE—The speed and power with which a shot is hit.

PERCENTAGE SHOT—The shot that is comfortable for the player to hit for a winner, especially if the opposing player is out of position

PLACEMENT—The intended destination of the ball being hit in the opposing player's court.

POACH—In doubles, the act of hitting a ball that would have been expected to go to one's partner.

POINT—The basic unit of scoring in a game. Once a server attempts to get a ball into the opposing court to begin the game, someone will win the point.

"PUSHER"—A player who does not hit the ball hard but keeps it in play.

RALLY—The act of hitting the ball back and forth between delivery of serve and the completion of the point.

READY POSITION — The position assumed by the receiver while he is awaiting his opponent's shot.

RECEIVER—The player who is awaiting his opponent's serve.

SERVE—The shot that a player hits to begin a point.

SERVER—The player who is hitting the serve.

SERVICE BOX — The rectangular area into which the server must hit the ball to begin the point. There is a right-hand service box and a left-hand service box on each side of the net.

SERVICE BREAK—When a server loses the serve.

SERVICE LINE—The line approximately halfway between the baseline and the net, running parallel to the net on each side of the court.

SET—A scoring unit. In conventional scoring, a set is won by the first player or team of players to win six games and be ahead by two games.

SIDELINES—The two outer boundary lines of the tennis court that run perpendicular to the net. Also referred to as the "doubles lines."

SINGLES—A game between two players, one on each side.

SITTER—A poor shot that "sits" in the air close to the net where the opponent has an easy opportunity to hit a winner.

SLICE—A stroke with any spin that is not topspin.

SMASH—A hard, overhead swing at the ball.

SPIN—The rotation applied to the ball by hitting it at an angle with the racket.

TOPSPIN—A stroke that imparts spin over the ball in the direction of flight.

VOLLEY — A shot wherein a player hits the ball before it strikes the ground.

WINNER—A shot hit into the opponent's court that is out of the reach of the opponent and therefore cannot be returned.

Appendices

Lest we forget that tennis is just a game and lest we take ourselves too seriously, I have included the following three appendices. While they are tongue-in-cheek, my guess is that each of us, from the beginner to the experienced player, will see aspects of ourselves that we need to laugh about.

The first appendix, "Tennis Double Talk," is a humorous guide that should help beginners understand what players mean by their *coded* statements—this will also be of help to experienced players.

The second appendix is a poem called "It's Tennis Elbow" that I hope will help you understand this most common physical ailment suffered by tennis players. Whether you have already experienced this disabling injury or not, you probably will, sooner or later. That's why I wrote the poem.

Remember, playing tennis is supposed to be fun. I hope this addendum will add a little humor that can help you put the game in proper perspective.

TENNIS DOUBLETALK

If you are a beginner at playing tennis, it is important that you devote some time to the study of the language of tennis as used by many tennis players. This is not a foreign language, but a message in code that may not be understood by the uninitiated. A study of this special tennis language will enable you to decipher the message in order to understand what your opponent is really saying, or more often, what he is not saying. It will also help you see more clearly what you are saying yourself.

Every segment of modern society has its own stock of shop-worn and cliché-ridden expressions. Few groups can match the supply of self-serving phrases and statements used by tennis players. This is because the average tennis player spends most of his court time being defeated by a few consistent winners. In order to protect his ego, the player accumulates a large inventory of ready-made statements (clichés) that can be used when he is ready to play, is playing, or has just played.

It is not surprising that after a few years, these statements become second nature and most players are not even aware of what they are saying. The beauty of this tennis language is its adaptability for use under all circumstances—by both winner and loser, young and old, male and female, and even by non-players.

It should be understood that the tennis language we are referring to does not use such words as "serve," "double-fault," "lob," "volley," "ace," etc. Those words are a part of the game and the meaning of each is quite specific (and is quite seriously defined in the Glossary). Tennis doubletalk expressions are not necessary to the playing of tennis and the meaning, when used by a tennis player, is often very different from the meaning given to the phrases by the uninformed listener.

Below are some of the more common *code* statements used by many tennis players. For your assistance, a clear translation follows each statement.

I don't think it's a good idea to play tennis with your wife.: My wife beats me every time we play.

June is afraid to play with me.: I'm such a poor player (or poor loser) that June refuses to play me.

I barely lost.: The score was 6-1, 6-1.

I won 6-1, 6-1.: I did, but I'm not going to tell you that my opponent had never played tennis before.

It was a riot.: I won 4-6, 7-5, 7-5.

The oversized widebody rackets should be outlawed.: An

eighty-year-old player with an oversized widebody racket beat me 6-2, 6-2.

I should have won.: I was lucky to win any points at all.

I didn't miss a single overhead yesterday.: It's true, but I hit only one overhead (hit it with the frame and it accidentally fell on the baseline).

I wasn't ready.: I got aced.

I got a terrible draw in the tournament.: Any place in the draw would have been terrible.

They wanted to rank me but I told them I wasn't interested.: Ranking committee never heard of him. He doesn't know that you must play in tournaments to receive a ranking.

It was out by two feet.: It was out by two inches.

I wish I had played pro tennis. I'd be a millionaire now.: Makes this statement only to those who have never seen him play.

I would never push my daughter to play tennis like some do.: Tried to get the daughter to play, but she had neither interest nor skill.

Never, but never, use a drop shot.: a) He cannot hit a drop shot.

b) He always loses to players who use drop shots.: *I usually have my racket strung at sixty-one and a half pounds.*

Trying to impress you. Couldn't tell whether his racket was strung at thirty or seventy pounds.: *I told Jimmy Connors. . .*

Nearest he ever was to Jimmy Connors was the 53rd row of the grandstand.: *Now, the reason McEnroe beat Borg was. . .*

Trying to impress you with his vast knowledge of tennis.: *If Borg had only listened to me. . .*

More bragging. Has only seen Borg on TV—and that was in black and white.: The above list is a partial guide to the more common tennis clichés. They should help you recognize the broader body for what they really are—contrived alibis used in an effort to defend the player's ego. If you should recognize some of these clichés as your own words, perhaps you should make an effort to eliminate them from your own tennis vocabulary. After all, it is just a game.

IT'S TENNIS ELBOW

It may not be as common as a cold,
when it grabs a hold.
It's tennis elbow.

It hits the elderly,
and teen, or in-between.
It's tennis elbow.

It may come from strain,
that incapacitating pain.
It's tennis elbow.

It may strike without warning,
while playing in the morning.
It's tennis elbow.

You may have it all the time,
or it may come and go.
It's tennis elbow.

There is no quick cure,
of this you can be sure.
It's tennis elbow.

If you've never had it, don't despair,
just wait, it will be there.
It's tennis elbow.

Index